AMBASSADORS FOR CHRIST

Peter Petroski

New Harbor Press
RAPID CITY, SD

Petroski/New Harbor Press
1601 Mt. Rushmore Rd. Ste 3288
Rapid City, SD 57701
www.NewHarborPress.com

Ordering Information:
Quantity sales. Special discounts are available on quantity purchases by corporations, associations, and others. For details, contact the "Special Sales Department" at the address above.

Ambassadors for Christ/Peter Petroski. -- 1st ed.
ISBN 978-1-63357-407-6

Ambassadors for Christ
1 Corinthians 5:17-20

Therefore, if anyone is in Christ, the new creation has come:[a] The old has gone, the new is here! All this is from God, who reconciled us to himself through Christ and gave us the ministry of reconciliation: that God was reconciling the world to himself in Christ, not counting people's sins against them. And he has committed to us the message of reconciliation. **We are therefore Christ's ambassadors,** *as though God were making his appeal through us. We implore you on Christ's behalf: Be reconciled to God.*

Contents

Forward

For God so loved the world (put your name in place of "the world"), that He gave His one and only Son (Jesus), that whoever (put your name in place of "whoever") believes in Him will not perish (die) but have eternal life.
John 3:16
OR reread and put your name in place of "the world" and "whoever."

* * * * *

It is humbling, a privilege, and a thrill to be part of God's process of Him saving people.

Almost 30 years ago on a typical Wednesday evening I'd sit in the back pew of the church with my pastor. Often, my pastor, Dan, would share about a relationship he was building with a man at the health club. We would pray for this man. Pastor Dan went to the club because he had back problems and he needed to exercise to build strength. As years went by Dan built a trusted relationship with this man. Pastor Dan was and is very concerned about people's souls and where they will spend eternity. Therefore, the reason we would pray.

The man we prayed for is the author of this book, Pete Petroski. A walking miracle. Pete is a dear friend now and most importantly a devout believer and follower of Jesus Christ. This book shares the details of Pete's journey.

You will see in the pages ahead how the Gospel (Good News) of Jesus transformed Pete's life and the lives of many others. My hope and prayer is, that as you read this book, if you are not a believer in Jesus, you would consider Him and what He has done for you. Death without Jesus means you will spend eternity in Hell. Hell, forever separation from God and Heaven. Stop, pause, and let that sink in.... Let Jesus change you and life will never be the same again. You can be the next walking miracle!

Gary Zimmerman

Introduction

This book is compiled with true stories mostly of people now living in Central Pennsylvania. They are examples of lives changed by Christ, who have matured to where they are embracing the Great Commission and sharing the Good News with others. The intention is not to entertain you or to display lives committed to serve. The purpose is to challenge you to listen to the whispering of the Holy Spirit and be faithful to God's plan for your life. Do you think living in the suburbs, owning two cars, going to church when it is convenient, is what God has in store for us?

If this book inspires you to pray about how God can use you, inspires you to search for ministry opportunities, or to start reading and studying your Bible.... then it was worth the work.

In my lifetime the world has changed dramatically! What is considered acceptable on TV, in relationships, what we call entertainment and how we spend our time are all different. Not all the changes are good! If you are a Christian reading this book, consider carefully how you spend your time and your money?

How much of your time is with God in a weeks' time compared to your time on Facebook or Twitter? How much of your resources are used to bless someone in need or tithing to your church? Food for thought!

This book is about lives who have been through different struggles, different addictions, different backgrounds. The similarity is how God changed our lives and is now using us to take what we have learned and help others (2 Timothy 2:2). My story is first, this is my written testimony of how Christ changed my life and what I am doing today. I have shared this at numerous Celebrate Recovery groups, most recently LCBC's Manheim campus. I also self-published a book titled, Metamorphosis the Final Edition which is on Barnes and Noble's site as an eBook. Print copy is available for $6 at psp50@yahoo.com which is my cost to print, anything above that amount goes to my 1X1 ministry with men in recovery. I will share briefly about my connection with each person's story, but I am only guiding the others, they are all coauthors of their own story. May God get all the Glory!

CHAPTER ONE

Pete Petroski

My name is Pete Petroski, I am a follower of Jesus Christ and a recovered alcoholic. I found the following quote written by Baptist pastor, Charles Spurgeon, this describes my life:

"But suppose a man can be so changed that just as freely as he was accustomed to curse he now delights to pray, and just as heartily as he hated religion, he now finds pleasure in it and just as earnestly as he sinned he now delights to be obedient to the Lord. This is a wonder, a miracle which only the grace of God can work, which gives God his highest glory".

I grew up in the Mechanicsburg area, in a kind of Ozzie & Harriet home, a dad, mother, brother in a middle-class development. Dad always had two jobs to make ends meet, so he was rarely home, he was a good example of a great work ethic.... but I would have rather had him spend more time with us at home. I started drinking with other kids in our neighborhood in my mid-teens stealing beer and cigarettes from our parent's homes.

When I graduated from HS, I had my first pot party which began a 20+ year habit of always having a bag of weed, smoking after work or all day on weekends. At the age of 17 I was arrested for the first time for underage drinking.

I wanted to leave home after High School and with a small inheritance, I was able to attend a business school in Minneapolis. I majored in partying the whole year and had a part time job mopping floors at night in a department store.

In early 1968 a group of us left Minneapolis and drove to Chicago because we heard the airlines at O'Hare Field in Chicago were hiring. The business school I was attending in Minneapolis taught courses on Transportation, so we were all hired by various airlines, I was hired by Delta Air Lines. We went back to Minneapolis, packed, and moved to Chicago. This became the worst time of my life, a good job, great money, but drinking, smoking pot, experimenting with LSD, all became routine. I was arrested for my first DUI in Chicago and the second arrest for underage drinking, I lost my license for a year. After two years in Chicago many of my friends were drafted to Viet Nam or moved home. I flunked my first Army physical in Chicago due to a high % of sugar in my blood, they said I was a borderline diabetic. This was due to the amount of whisky I was drinking daily.

I moved back to Pennsylvania, reconnected with my High School drinking friends, and made contacts for a regular supply of pot. I was hired by an Insurance Company as a claim's adjuster trainee and soon after, I got married. In 1973 I got my second DUI-on Rt 83 in York driving south in the northbound lanes in broad daylight, I lost my license again for a year. I did not drive the entire year except for the night my wife went into labor with our daughter and I drove her to the Hospital and left my car there.

For the next 15 years, I moved upward in my Insurance career, several promotions, transfers/moves, my focus was all about making money, as much as possible. My Insurance jobs changed from claims adjuster to marketing rep, eventually to Regional Marketing VP. One of my responsibilities was entertaining clients and my expense account paid for everything...Dinner, drinks, weed or whatever. I was running a $50 million-dollar region, making the Company more money than any other territory countrywide, which gave me lots of freedom. As my job responsibilities increased, I had to spend more time building relationships with large accounts, including taking regular trips with clients to the Caribbean and our wives were never invited. The trips included lots of drinking and whatever the client wanted to keep their business.

In 1992 my life started to crash, I was making lots of $ as Branch manager & VP of a wholesale insurance agency and driving a Mercedes they were paying for, I was very successful in the worlds view...but inside, I was miserable. I left my first wife and daughter and moved into an apartment my Employer owned.

A few years prior, I met a guy at a health club who asked me about my walk with the Lord, I blew him off and turns out later I found out he was a pastor. Occasionally guys from work invited me to church, I always declined, as they were the same guys drinking and smoking pot with me on Monday so why be a hypocrite like them?

In January 1993 I met a lady named Brenda during a hike with the York Hiking Club. I could tell by her car and clothes; she did not make a lot of money. This was how I measured people, what do you own? How much money do you make? But she had a sense of peace and joy that I could not understand. She was raising two teenage girls, was working at a local Nursing Home, and drove a 15+ year old car.... how could she be happy? Then she told me about her relationship with Jesus Christ. My first reaction was Oh no, another Jesus freak, but I was curious, and we started dating and nine months later we were married.

However, she said when we got married, I had to go to church, I agreed and one of the first we visited was the Church where the guy I met at the health club was the Pastor, the York Grace Brethren Church. The first time I was overwhelmed, I felt like he was pointing at me during his message. I told Brenda, boy he sure got carried away! At the time he would not perform our wedding since we were both divorced. We decided to go to Olympic National Park outside Seattle to get married in October of 93.

Back home, we started visiting other churches and we ended up at YGBC. Brenda wanted to rededicate her life to Christ and get baptized. Pastor Dan came to our home to explain Baptism, I also wanted to be baptized so I listened as well. I had recently asked Jesus to come into my life but told no one until this time.

I still had to deal with drinking, and I knew I could not quit on my own, I tried many times. I was drinking less now and had given up Pot about 5 years prior. My incentive here was drug testing, I was concerned this would have an impact with keeping my job. A few weeks after accepting Christ, I was out drinking again and came out of a bar and got into my car to drive home. I now understand what it means to be convicted by the HS because as I sat there in my car, I remembered I used to call my friends hypocrites who invited me to church and on Monday we were out after work in the bars. As I sat there, I asked Christ to forgive me and take away the desire to ever drink again and I committed to serve Him forever. Last month was 26 years of being sober and free!

After giving my life to Christ, we started attending York GBC on Sunday mornings, Sunday evenings, and Wed nights, I started being discipled by Pastor Dan that I had originally met at the Health Club and this continued for the next 15 years.

Not long after I stopped drinking, I had to figure out how to explain to my employer I could no longer take those trips to the Caribbean with clients, I was not drinking at all! Brenda & I were coming up on our first anniversary and a Company sponsored trip to the Caribbean came up for my clients. I told my employer I would pay for my wife to go...they refused so I did too. I could no longer do some of the things my job required of me...so January 1st, 1995 I was fired from my great paying job and escorted from the office. A month later I was hired by JOB-a Christian Insurance Agency specializing in insuring Churches, Christian Schools and Camps. I started at the bottom making less than half what I had been making...I was told God that would provide, and He did.

It was not an easy transition; it was humbling to transition from working with million-dollar+ clients and partying in the Caribbean to answering phones taking claims and learning about insuring Churches.

Brenda and I were growing spiritually, I was asked to lead the Mission Commission at Church, we had been on two mission trips, Western Europe, and Chile. We moved to downtown York in a row house near the YMCA wondering how God would use us. Soon we found we were surrounded by crack houses, street people, and homeless; God started using us in that neighborhood. I gave free haircuts, we were praying on the streets with strangers, getting people off the streets into the mission, serving at the YMCA, and getting addicts into rehab programs. I was watching God was take my hurts, habits and hang ups to help others.

In 2003 we moved to Columbia. Not knowing what God had in store for us here, we went through a Church Planters assessment process In Washington State and upon returning, we started New Vision Church in Columbia in 2005. Our Bible studies were split up between men and women and God kept sending us people struggling with addictions. I searched online and found Celebrate Recovery (CR) in Millersville, I took one of my guys and I loved it, it was too religious for him. I brought my wife Brenda and we started attending together every week for months. In December 2006 we opened CR in Columbia, thanks to encouragement from Frank & Sharon from Millersville CR. Our Church plant turned into a Friday night recovery ministry and God did some amazing things. In 2013 we came along side another Church plant called Vision Columbia, a Mennonite church. Eventually I became Pastor of Prison and Recovery ministries. I was visiting men in both York and Lancaster County prisons. We had a great group of CR leaders, Scott-was on that team. In 2014 I retired from working full time work at JOB, but continued PT from home another 2 years. May of 2016, we closed CR in Columbia as we felt God nudging us to move on.

My passion today is 1 x 1 discipleship meetings with men. A few are in prison and God keeps opening doors for more opportunities. I work PT at the Auto Auction in East Petersburg and as Chaplain at several Lancaster County businesses.

October 2018, I traveled to VN on a mission trip, one of my roles was to meet a neurosurgeon in Saigon who started some recovery houses, he wanted to discuss Faith Based Recovery. I sent him my testimony to translate and I was able to share my story @ a recovery house in Saigon. He has a 90%+ recovery rate based on a commitment to live in the house and study the Bible for two years. I gave him some CR materials and I understand there is CR interest in Hanoi. If you are a VN Vet, Bob Smoker is the man I will travel with, he was there during the war and has been back over 15 times.

So, what does it take to stay in recovery... a personal relationship with Jesus Christ is the foundation of my life and recovery. Also, Daily Bible reading, at least one accountability partner, get involved in a church, and attendance in a faith-based recovery meeting like CR, and **please join a Step study**! The Daily Bread devo became an inspiration to me and our leaders to encourage us to read through the Bible in a year and hold each other accountable to daily Bible reading.

This year I published my story titled: Metamorphosis the Final Edition, available at Barnes and Noble's web site as an eBook. Another great way to share your story! I recently printed copies as well. I have a few tonight if anyone is interested.

I have lived a full life, traveled a lot, lived at about 30 different places, had 10 jobs, sailed throughout the Caribbean &

became a certified scuba diver, hiked all over the US and the Western highlands of Scotland, The Andes in southern Chile. I have owned lots of toys and loved making money. **But** nothing has been as rewarding or as satisfying as the last 20 years serving Jesus Christ. It is not about what I have at the end of life, it is about who I am and how I have served. Jesus Christ took away my desire to drink, I gave Him my life and will continue serving Him until I go home. Today I also serve as Assoc Pastor @ Community Cornerstone Church in York and work for Marketplace Chaplains.

As I said in the beginning when I quoted Charles Spurgeon, **"This is a wonder, a miracle which only the Grace of God can work".**

CHAPTER TWO

Ryan & Lisa Smith

I met Ryan at an event their church sponsors each year at Cherry Lane in York, Pa. It was a ministry to homeless and street people in York, offered a free meal, free haircuts, Christian music from several venues including Ransome Soul from York. It was an all-day event with baptisms on site open to the public and I witnessed at least 6 people dunked. There were several testimonies shared including Ryan's story and he shared briefly about their Tuesday night ministry as well. I asked for more info later and my wife and I started coming to minister to the people who came for food and fellowship. At this time, it was cold as I started coming in December, we had many a cold windy night offering food and fellowship to the one who came. I asked Ryan and Lisa to write a testimony of how Christ changed their lives, read on.

Testimony of Ryan & Lisa Smith

Pastors Ryan & Lisa Smith are husband and wife, and they were joined together to devote their lives to pursuing the Lord. They were both rescued by the Lord from lifestyles of addictions to a variety of vices, and were filled with His Spirit, to be witnesses of the transforming love and power of Jesus Christ.

Ryan & Lisa now carry a vision to lead a people who want to know Jesus and follow Him everywhere He leads us. Ryan & Lisa both Pastor and serve in a leadership capacity at Great Reward Ministries.

Ryan's Early Years

Ryan lost his father at the age of 5, due to a car accident. His mother raised him to the best of her ability. However, not having a father to pass down what is needed for a boy to become a man left Ryan with a lot of unanswered questions and unfulfilled needs of his heart. In Ryan's early teens, drugs and alcohol seemed to fill the voids and ease the pain. However, as Ryan grew older, drugs and alcohol became more of a priority and his path became more destructive. Failing as a father, son, and friend, drug rehabs, crime, and incarceration became a story that Ryan never dreamed for his life. Ryan tried many times to fight and walk away from his addictions, but the result was always failure. Although Ryan was not raised in church, he had heard a lot of talk about God while he was growing up. However, in the spring of 2001, in a Bible study in the York County Prison, Tom Fredrick shared the gospel in a way that inspired Ryan to go back to his cell and cry out to God to make him a new man. Jesus met Ryan's request with the power of His Spirit, removed the bondage of his addiction, and showed him that God was his Father. At 27 years old, not only was Ryan born again and free from drug addiction, but now he had the Father that his broken heart longed for over 20 years.

Ryan was released from prison straight into a Christian men's ministry house called Glory House Ministry. Tom Fredrick was the director of the men's house and the pastor of Glory House Church. It was here that Ryan spent the next eight years of his life learning to be a godly man, serve the Lord, and was discipled to be the leader that God was calling him to be. In the beginning of Ryan's walk with Jesus, he had a lot of fear that he would go back to his old lifestyle if he did not get this new life "right." However, the Lord showed Ryan through 2 Corinthians 5:17 that He completely transformed him into a brand-new Ryan and that he would never be the old Ryan again. The life of drug addict is very predictable. They spend all their time thinking about themselves. However, being set free through God's grace and power, learning to submit to authority, living a life for God's glory and not his own agenda, not only changed Ryan spiritually, but cleansed him from his old stinking thinking and addictive behaviors.

Lisa's Early Years

Lisa was raised by a single mother. She never knew her father. Her mother suffered from a broken heart, for various reasons, which lead to extreme sadness and depression. Lisa experienced a lot of dysfunction in the home at an early age. Lisa longed to know her father and to be loved. Lisa's sister ran away from home at the age of 16 and her mother was hospitalized for a lengthy time. Lisa suffered from a broken heart and abandonment issues because of the circumstances of her life. Lisa lived with family members during this time, but as an escape from the pain and brokenness in her heart, she began to give herself to drugs and alcohol. This was a vice she used to drown out the pain. Lisa lived a promiscuous lifestyle, looking for love in all the wrong places. Lisa attracted the wrong kind of men that were not looking out for her best interest. At the age of 16, she became pregnant with her 1st son and gave birth soon after. The father of the child was absent from their lives, and Lisa once again was alone, abandoned and rejected. Through Lisa's promiscuous lifestyle, she became pregnant 3 more times; 2 ended in abortions and her final pregnancy resulted in the birth of her 2nd son. Lisa felt as if no one would ever want her based on the decisions she made in her life. She married her 2nd sons father knowing deep down the relationship was destructive. The marriage did not last, and Lisa ended up raising 2 boys on her own at a very young age. Her sons' father was in and out of their life, struggled with severe addiction and was incarcerated most of the time. Lisa's lifestyle led to run-ins with the legal system and near-death experiences. Addiction consumed Lisa's life until she came to an end of herself. At one point, Lisa felt like she was going to die while using drugs. She cried out to the Lord for His help. That is when Lisa had an encounter with the one and only true and living God. Jesus set her free instantly from drug and alcohol addiction and she knew that He met her right where she was at. In her mess. She had not done anything right, He just loved her enough to save her.

Lisa knew she had to walk away from her old life. She left friends and everything that so easily ensnared her. Lisa set herself apart unto the Lord. Lisa did not have anyone to teach her how to walk with the Lord. After her encounter, she began to cling to the word of God as life. Whatever the word said, that is what Lisa did. It was through His Spirit, and the revelation of the word, that freedom began to come. One of the scriptures that was significant in Lisa life was "submit to God, resist the devil and he will flee." Over time, and standing in faith through the word, Lisa's life was being transformed. There were many wrong mindsets that gripped Lisa's life and one by one the Lord began to strip her of those bondages. Lisa gave the Lord the place in her heart where she gave to so many others in her past; that place where she longed to be loved. As He filled her with His love, she wept and healed the very brokenness inside her. During these early years with the Lord, Lisa gave herself only to Him. It was not until 6 years later that the Lord brought Ryan her future husband into her life.

Becoming One

In 2006, Ryan and Lisa met in a prayer group. They realized early on that they had the same passions for the Lord and similar testimonies. They both lived lives devoted to serving God and desired to see Him transform the lives of others. Their hearts burned with passion to see the lost and broken become faithful sons and daughters of the living God. While Ryan and Lisa faithfully served in the church, they felt most alive on the streets of York City. Seeing the power of the Holy Spirit move through people's lives, by sharing the gospel on the streets, started to change them to the point they began to see that this was part of His purpose for joining them together. Ryan and Lisa's hearts ache to love those that are marginalized and suffering from the very things that entangled their lives.

After getting married in 2007, Ryan and Lisa had many trials and tribulations. Many years of hardship and sickness plagued their lives. They were misunderstood by family, friends and even the church. They remained faithful to God through these seasons. They learned how to stay committed to their marriage vows no matter what difficulties life brought. The very purpose of the call of God on their lives is what gave them strength to endure these extreme difficulties. Even though they were discouraged at times, the passion for loving Jesus and others never faded. It is through these hardships that God has etched His wisdom and character into the very fabric of their hearts. God's vision and purpose for their lives has grown beyond just the two of them. They are a three-strand cord that is not easily broken.

Ryan and Lisa now pastor a small church in Wrightsville, PA. It was established upon Philippians 2:1-11 and Isaiah 61 and its purpose is to raise up a generation of passionate Jesus people, empty of their own agendas and ambitions, and in pursuit of advancing the Kingdom of God for the glory of Jesus! We love the one that God places in front of us. We love each person right where they are at and believe in them until they can believe in themselves.

Ryan and Lisa have also established a street ministry in York City that reaches out to those that are broken, addicted, homeless and generally marginalized by society. It is in this very place that we feel most alive and the closes to Jesus.

CHAPTER THREE

Jeremy Grant

I met Jeremy about 5-6 years ago when he showed up at one of our Friday night Celebrate Recovery meetings in Columbia. We started by meeting one time to see what kind of connection we made, and it never stopped. We started with Measure of a Man by Gene Getz and have gone through numerous books. Jeremy has been my favorite amongst many men I have mentored over the years, he always does the lesson and has been willing to step outside his comfort zone and grow in his walk with the Lord. Here is his story:

I grew up in a broken home. My mother and father both delt in substance abuse. There was often verbal and mental abuse between the two that had gotten so bad at times that I would be sent away to my aunts for the summer. Throughout my youth I would watch my dad go through multiple relapses. At age 13 I would begin my own experimentation with marijuana, alcohol, and hallucinogens. At age 17 I was introduced to narcotics by my father which eventually would lead into full on addiction to pain medication. At age 18 my dad died of a morphine overdose; I was the one who discovered him which sent me into a dark descent into what I would call my own personal hell. I received ailments ... Depression, anxiety, PTSD, and social phobias. 3 years later my mother died of walking pneumonia, she was bulimic and was unable to recover. As I dove deeper into my addictions, I would become homeless for 2 years, do time in prison for a DUI and narcotics. As a non-believer, I hated life, hated people and was suicidal, I did not want to live. I eventually dabbled in heroin and began to sell opiates. I was lost, hopeless and without love. My older sister would be the next in line as a victim of addiction that would take her life. At the end of my rope, I would go out one last time to get drunk and high ... Unbeknownst to me ... The following morning, I would awake to a pull from something not of me ... A desire to go to church. That morning I gave half of my heart to Christ. It was not until weeks later I would receive another desire ... A desire to surrender 100 % to Christ ... By dying to myself. All I was and all I possessed ... I threw away ... Music, movies, t shirts ... Everything that posed as an idol. At this time something strange happened ... I went to sleep and awoke the next morning changed ... New desires, a new mind ... No withdrawals, no programs ... No detox ... Just Jesus Christ. From that moment on. I would be changed forever. I was baptized by my mentor Peter petroski and would begin discipleship with him, I would Make church a priority, spend time in the Word daily, share my testimony at Manos House (a juvenile detention center) & church. I had later found out that family members had been praying for me for years. Prayers that I would no longer embrace the darkness and that Jesus would fill me with His light. He answered ...My name is Jeremy Grant; I've been walking with Christ now for 6 yrs ... I was delivered through intercessory prayer which led to a divine intervention with my Maker. I once was lost but now am found ... Once a non-believer but now I truly believe!

CHAPTER FOUR

Dr Thanh Tran

I met Dr Thanh while in Vietnam in 2018 on a Mission trip with Bob Smoker and Gary Zimmerman, both from our church, Community Cornerstone Church in York, Pa. Prior to going to Vietnam I was not sure about even going as I had nothing to contribute except to build relationships with the contacts Bob and Gary made in their prior trips. A few weeks prior to leaving Bob had been talking to Dr Thanh and told him about my background with addiction and a ministry called Celebrate Recovery. My wife Brenda and I started this in Columbia Pa in 2006 and closed in May 2016. Long story short his Dr Thanh heard about Celebrate Recovery and he invited me to share my testimony at one of his recovery houses in Saigon while we were visiting. I agreed and sent him m story weeks prior and he translated it to Vietnam so he could translate during my sharing. I later determined his recovery house were only focused on a 2-year commitment to stay in the house and study the Bible and his recovery rate was 95%! This was higher than any other residential recovery facility I had encountered up until that time. Here is his story first in English than Vietnamese.

Being born into a poor family in a rural area in central Vietnam, I am aware of the poverty of farmers. I grew up during the war in Vietnam between the US military and the Communist regime in North Vietnam. I witnessed death all around me during my young years and fortunately, when I was 5, the war ended. However, the years after the war were extremely difficult days of economic starvation in a backward communist regime, within a month, it was like stepping back into a more backward world. a hundred years. Not only poverty, the oppression and loss of freedom in the communist regime is the worst mental repression. After looking back, I can see that these are the visits that have taught me the most in my life. Through years of poverty and my family's land being confiscated, I realized that only education could help me get out of this scourge. I was determined to do well in school to hope for a stable career, although at that time those who went to school properly, would not have a better income than those who did not go to school, but I still recognized that the future of the country would change but cannot last forever.

Since entering high school I had to work hard with my parents to make a living, I have worked with my father to reclaim wasteland to cultivate. However, because of a clear goal, I tried to study well and focused on learning what I needed to achieve my goals. As a result, after high school, I had to take a college exam. I had to study extremely hard (that is the difference between the education of Vietnam and Europe and America). My biggest passion for the future is that I wanted to become an engineer but since few students after finishing high school could immediately pass the entrance exam to Polytechnic University, so I did not dare to take the exam. I entered a polytechnic university and took another exam, which is an economics university, to try my hand. I passed this exam and continued to attend the University of Economics, Ho Chi Minh City. The irony is that I never thought I would study economics and did not like this industry very much, but since I took the exam, I had to study. After two months of studying, I felt this was the wrong subject for me, so I decided to drop out. Most of my friends who could afford to stay in Ho Chi Minh City, did so to prepare for the exam next year, but because of my family's difficult situation, I went back home to practice for the next year.

Every day, seeing my diligence and determination, my dad used to tell me that if there was an engineer and a doctor in the house, he would still prefer a doctor. My father is illiterate because he did not have an education and did not understand that engineers and doctors are two completely different disciplines. The entrance exams are also different, so he always told me, you should take the medical exam. In fact, at that time, getting into medicine was much more difficult than getting into Bach Khoa. At that time, I knew I was facing a difficult choice, but because of my love, I decided that by doing his grandfather's wishes, I had to re-take new subjects to take the medical exam. Fortunately, that year I passed into medicine with a very high score. Entering medical school has been an extremely difficult journey for me as it costs a lot of money to buy books and materials while my parents are extremely poor and have no money to support me while I studied. I worked part-time almost full time to have money to pay for living and school expenses. Then six years of medicine passed. One thing that I always thank God for is that medical school itself is where I found God. When I entered to medical school, I did not believe in what I learned before, which was the Darwinian theory of evolution. I am always trying to find out about the Creator of the universe; I studied many different religions such as Buddhism, Islam, Cao Dai, Catholicism and Protestantism. Each religion offered their own explanation for creation. In the end I came across the clearest and most complete explanation from a pastor of the Vietnamese Protestant Church (South). Scripture convinced me at that time, I decided to accept God as my Savior and join the Southern Vietnamese evangelical congregation in 1990.

At that time, Vietnam was a country with a long Buddhist tradition and was also heavily influenced by Confucianism and Taoism from China. So, believing in God and following the Protestant Church is seen as leaving family and forsaking his ancestors. At this time, the relationship between Vietnam and the US was not good, Protestantism was the religion of America and was often considered to have political involvement. However, as a self-seeker to God, I walked with God powerfully and was not affected by anything. Then the news of my receiving God and going to the Protestant church reached the ears of my father back home, and he managed to contact me and suggested that I come home. Receiving a message from an acquaintance, I understood that a big problem was facing me. When I returned to the hometown as suggested by my father and I immediately met my father first. I looked at his face that was filled with anger. My dad did not say anything but gave me two options. The first was I must immediately quit following God and come back to my family; He declared if I did not fulfill my promise, he would never see me as his child again. The second is if I continue to follow my Lord, he will drink a bottle of poison already on the table for me to witness his death. At that time, I faced a situation where I felt unable to make a choice. I closed my eyes for a few seconds and listened to the Lord's voice, I immediately realized one thing God told me was to postpone a decision and I will help you. I suddenly thought of a third option and asked my dad's permission to give him a few words and my father agreed. I started to say. Dad, I love you very much and as you can see, I have tried my best to study so I would not betray you. Since I now follow God, He teaches me to honor my parents, and that is one of the 10 commandments of God. So, I will not be able to choose right now, please give me another option, that is a month away and I will choose one of the two choices you have given. Since this is an important issue in my life, I need to think carefully. This means in a month; I will be deciding to choose one of the two options you made for me. Strangely, my father accepted my proposal and had no other response. I went back to school to study and thought about how to answer but I had no guidance from God. I wondered, but the time had come, so I returned to my hometown to decide about my option. However, I had absolute peace because I believed God would act with the problem that could not be resolved a month ago. I got home at dusk and was carefully coming into the house, when my dad opened the door and said "baby!" My dad's gentle voice confused me. Suddenly my dad got on his knees and told me, "Son, pray for me to follow my Lord." I still do not understand what happened, but with great joy I knelt with my father and prayed for him to accept Jesus as his Savior.

After I finished praying, I regained my composure and asked my father why he had changed his mind. "He decided to follow my god because he was too afraid of God," he said. In the past month, a lot of incidents happened in my family that made my dad want to collapse, many times in the past month he thought of dying because of a brother of mine who was the principal of a school. Three times my brother threatened to kill my father for unimportant reasons. He did not understand why my brother showed such attitude and yet, another younger brother has been gambling and lost all his money and has sold all his property to pay off his debt. This has before never happened in my family. Right now, my father compared what I did for the family that he left his ancestors, and he regretted his accusations. He thought of the God I was honoring. Worshiping God has the supernatural power that controls everything that is happening. He thought of my delaying a decision to let God act and if he continued against God, how dreadful God's punishment would be, so he decided to follow God and seek his forgiveness.

Ever since my father accepted the Lord, he has encountered persecution and it came from a brother of his, my uncle, who had been a Communist for many years and is still an active member of the Communist party. My uncle warned me many times about following my God, but since I was his nephew and went to school far from home, he could not see me. But with my father they met often and the first thing he advised my father was to give up his religion immediately. At this time, my father faced a difficult choice like me, to obey his son and follow God and or listening to his brother and leave God. However, he still believed in my decision, so he tried to delay my uncle. From here on out, I began to pray for my uncle every day. Every time we met, we were happy with each other, but he always reminded me to give up following God because the gospel is American. I have repeatedly explained to him now that the relationship between Vietnam and the US is progressing very well and the past war has receded into the past. Besides, Protestantism is not an American religion but comes from Judaism. Three years later, my father returned to God after a stroke. My uncle continued to live for another 10 years. For these 10 years I tried to see my uncle once a year to talk About God to him. One summer day 2007 I received a phone call from a son of my uncle who told me that my uncle was in critical condition in the hospital and would probably not die now but he kept reminding him to call me to say that he is about to die and he wants me to be there to pray for him. However, this younger brother was just the one delivering the message, not knowing what he meant to pray. I told my younger brother, "I don't know, but you already know what your father wants you to pray for."

I firmly believe that he wanted to receive the Lord before he left this world. But at that time, I was very busy with the Church's work, so I could not visit my uncle because it was in the central area 1000 km away from Saigon. But I told my brother that you can rest assured, I will pray and believe that your father will get over this time and that your father will only die after seeing you again. My younger brother was incredibly surprised at what I said. But my uncle healed and returned home to the surprise of many in the hospital. Three months later I decided to go to see my uncle and pray for him. On the way I continued to receive another phone call from my brother, and he said that my uncle was seriously ill and was admitted to the hospital, so I suggested that I see him soon. I said, I was on my way and would come that night. I arrived that evening, but it was too late to visit him in the hospital, so I stayed at a hotel near my uncle's house. At 3:00 the next morning I received another phone call from our brother, who said that my uncle had been brought home be-cause his family wanted him to die at home, so the hospital gave him oxygen to take home. I rushed past his house and when I entered the house, I saw people crying because he was lying in a coma as if he were dead. When I entered, my uncle's son hit him and said loudly in his ear "Anh Thanh has come". The strange thing everyone saw was that he opened his eyes and looked at me intently. I knelt down at his bed and told him, "I think I won't have much time to explain to you, but I'm sure you understand everything and now let me pray for you to accept God. " I prayed and he spoke my words very clearly, surprising everyone around him. After I finished praying, I told him, "Now please be quiet so I pray for you to go to heaven with God. Two minutes after my prayer he was officially out of this world and I am sure he is in heaven with the Lord right now. My years in medical school were the years when I participated in many Church activities to reach the poor. I have led many doctors to visit poor areas, up to 100 such trips over the years. When I graduated in 1996, I wondered whether I had to return to my hometown to work or to stay in Saigon to have a better chance of serving God. I decided to stay in Saigon to work for a Korean medical ministry in Saigon then four years later I decided to move to World Vision. The job here was very good, I was promoted a lot, but I was not satisfied because it was a very large Christian organization but closely watched by the government, so I felt very claustrophobic. From there I thought I needed to do something different and decided to look for a scholarship to study theology. My fate came and I received a theology graduate scholarship to study in America. After three years of study and practice I thanked God and have always questioned why God allowed me to practice at different ministry that is for addicts in prison in Yakima, Washington. During my internship here, I became interested in drug addicts. The leader here wanted me to stay to help them for a long time, but I firmly answered that I had to go back to Vietnam because God called me to help the Vietnamese back home. I returned to Vietnam and was accepted by the Southern Vietnam Protestant Congregation to work for them at the General Conference's headquarters in Saigon. I started to build a new committee, the Social Health Committee, to begin helping the church openly and officially out into the community. We used to do it in the past but only worked in the "shadow and publicity" of the government. Now we have decided to step out of the light to do this and it was a huge step forward for the church in Vietnam. We have done a lot of community projects and have given the local congregation a great influence on the community through which the name of God may be glorified. A very big thing that I have done is that I formed a medical team of over 100 Protestant doctors working in Medical Missions for poor areas and we reached out to patients in all parts of the country. However, one thing that of concern is we only treat patients with common illnesses but are not allowed to consult and communicate with patients because they are afraid of us evangelizing. So, I pray to God that He will empower me to reach out to fully consult patients. And I realized that to do this, only when I could visit the hospital the hospital's people would have to do it. But sadly, if I were an employee of the hospital, then I was strictly managed and would not have the opportunity to talk about God or to counsel the patient comprehensively. I keep praying to God for a solution because I have been working for 10 years in the Protestant Church of Vietnam in the South. God immediately answered by connecting me with the Cure International organization. I know this is God's will and I have accepted to work for this organization. This is a specialized organization of neurosurgery for children with hydrocephalus (Hydrocephalus) and cerebrospinal drainage (Spina Bifida).

We have a Memorandum of Understanding with hospitals that is exactly what I want is that we support the hospital to train endoscopists (in Uganda) for these two diseases and support for the disease. They allow us when in the hospital to advise patients in a comprehensive way and this is an opportunity for our patients to see the love of God through our work. Currently, I have worked with the 3 largest pediatric hospitals in Vietnam which are in Saigon, Da Nang and Hanoi. In addition, I am responsible for managing many other hospitals in Asia.

God has responded to me twice as much as I asked for, that is work at a hospital in Hanoi where I could share God with many patients and associating with local churches to open new churches. I have always asked God since my return to Vietnam in 2006, "why did God put me in an internship in a drug addiction ministry?" I sought drug addiction ministry in Vietnam in 2016, a large door opened for myself and I have started to help detoxification centers in Vietnam since 2016. I thank God every day we can improve on the organizational management of this ministry. And to this day the Vietnamese government, despite deliberately refusing and disapproving this work of the Church, sees that our having great success. We have discussed the government consider providing us with a license to officially operate the entire territory of Vietnam.

Được sinh ra trong một gia đình nghèo tại một vùng quê ở miền Trung của Việt Nam tôi ý thức được sự nghèo khó của người nông dân. Đặc biệt, tôi lớn lên ngay trong thời buổi chiến tranh ở Việt Nam giữa quân đội Mỹ và chế độ Cộng sản tại miền Bắc Việt Nam. Tôi được chứng kiến được cảnh chết chóc đầy dẫy xung quanh mình trong những năm tháng còn rất nhỏ và may thay, khi tôi lên 5 thì chiến tranh cũng kết thúc. Tuy nhiên, những năm tháng sau chiến tranh là những chuỗi ngày cực kỳ khó khăn đói kém về kinh tế trong một chế độ cộng sản lạc hậu, chỉ trong vòng 1 tháng, tôi giống như bước lùi vào một cái thế giới lạc hậu hơn cả trăm năm. Không chỉ nghèo khó thôi, sự áp bức và mất quyền tự do trong chế độ CS mới là một sự đàn áp tồi tệ nhất về tinh thần. Sau này nhìn lại tôi mới thấy rằng đây chính là những thăm năm tháng dạy dỗ tôi nhiều nhất trong cuộc đời. Trãi qua năm tháng đói khổ và ruộng đất của gia đình tôi bị tịch thu hết, tôi ý thức được, chỉ có học hành mới giúp tôi thoát được hoang cảnh này. Tôi quyết tâm học hành thật giỏi để mong có được một nghề nghiệp ổn định mặc dù lúc đó người đi học đàng hoàng thì ra trường đi làm cũng chưa chắc có thu nhập khá hơn người không đi học là bao nhiêu nhưng tôi vẫn nhìn nhận được rằng tương lai của đất nước rồi cũng sẽ thay đổi chứ không thể kéo dại như thế mãi.

Từ khi bước vào cấp ba tôi đã phải lao động cực nhọc cùng với cha mẹ của mình để kiếm sống qua ngày, tôi đã cùng với bố mình để đi khai khẩn đất hoang để trồng trọt. Tuy nhiên vì có một mục tiêu rõ ràng nên tôi đã cố gắng học thật giỏi và tập trung vào học những gì mình cần đạt được mục tiêu mà thôi, Kết quả là sau khi học xong cấp ba tôi phải trải qua một kỳ thi đại học cực kỳ khó khăn (đó là cái khác biệt giữa nền giáo dục của Việt Nam và các nước Âu Mỹ). Đam mê lớn nhất của tôi cho tương lai là tôi muốn trở thành một kỹ sư nhưng vì thời đó ít có sinh viên nào sau khi học xong cấp ba có thể thi đỗ thẳng vào đại học Bách Khoa ngay, vì vậy tôi không dám thi vào đại học bách khoa mà lại thi một trường khác đó là trường đại học kinh tế để thử sức của mình. Kỳ thi này, tôi đã đỗ vào trường đại học kinh tế thành phố Hồ Chí Minh. Một sự trớ trêu thay đó là tôi chưa bao giờ nghĩ mình sẽ học kinh tế và cũng không thích ngành này lắm nhưng vì đã thi rồi nên tôi phải theo học. Vào học được hai tháng tôi cảm nhận được tôi đây là ngành học không đúng với tôi vì vậy tôi quyết định bỏ học. Phần lớn bạn bè của tôi có điều kiện thì ở lại tại thành phố Hồ Chí Minh để luyện thi cho năm sau nhưng vì hoàn cảnh gia đình của tôi khó khăn nên tôi phải quay trở về nhà tự luyện thi cho năm sau.

Hằng ngày, thấy sự cần mẫn và quyết tâm của tôi bố tôi thường hay nói với tôi rằng nếu trong nhà có một người kỹ sư và một bác sĩ thì bố của tôi vẫn thích bác sĩ hơn. Bố của tôi là người không biết chữ vì không được học hành từ nhỏ nên ông cũng không hiểu được kỹ sư và bác sĩ là hai ngành học hoàn toàn khác nhau, tức là môn thi vào cũng khác nhau, vì vậy ông hay bảo tôi con nên thi vào y khoa. Thật sự vào thời điểm đó thi vào y khoa khó hơn vào Bách Khoa rất nhiều. Lúc đấy tôi biết mình đứng trước một sự chọn lựa rất khó khăn nhưng vì thương bố của tôi nên tôi quyết định là làm theo ý của ông tôi phải dành thời gian để học lại những môn học mới để thi vào y khoa. Thật may mắn năm đó tôi đã đỗ vào y khoa với số điểm rất cao. Bước chân vào học y khoa là một chặng đường cực kỳ khó khăn đối với tôi vì học y khoa tốn kém rất nhiều tiền cho việc mua sách vở và tài liệu học trong khi đó cha mẹ của tôi lại rất nghèo và không có tiền để chu cấp cho tôi ăn học. Tôi phải đi làm thêm gần như kín thời gian để có tiền trang trải cho việc sinh sống và học tập. Thế rồi Sáu năm y khoa cũng trôi qua. Một điều mà tôi luôn tạ ơn Chúa đó là chính trường y khoa là nơi tôi biết đến Chúa. Khi tôi bước chân vào học y khoa tôi không tin vào những gì mà tôi đã học trước đó, là học thuyết tiến hóa Darwin. Tôi luôn cố gắng đi tìm cho hiểu về Đấng Tạo Hóa ra vũ trụ này; tôi đi tìm hiểu rất nhiều tôn giáo khác nhau như Phật giáo, Hồi giáo, Cao đài, Công Giáo và Tin Lành. Mỗi tôn giáo, tôi nhận ra được lời giải thích của họ cho sự tạo hóa. Cuối cùng tôi gặp được lời giải thích rõ ràng và đầy đủ nhất là bởi một mục sư của Hội Thánh Tin Lành Việt Nam (Miền nam). Lời Kinh thánh đã thuyết phục tôi trong lúc đó, tôi quyết định tiếp nhận

Chúa làm Cứu Chúa của mình và gia nhập vào hội thánh tin lành Việt Nam miền Nam vào năm 1990.

Lúc bấy giờ, Việt Nam là một đất nước có truyền thống Phật giáo từ lâu đời và cũng bị ảnh hưởng nặng nề bởi nho giáo và lão giáo từ Trung Quốc. Vì vậy việc tin nhận Chúa và theo bên Hội thánh Tin lành được xem như là bỏ ông, bỏ bà và bỏ tổ tiên của mình. Đặc biệt, vào thời điểm này mối quan hệ giữa Việt Nam và Mỹ chưa tốt, đạo Tin Lành được xem là đạo của Mỹ và thường mặc nhiên được xem có dính dáng đến chính trị. Tuy nhiên, là một người tự tìm đến với Chúa, tôi bước đi với Chúa cách mạnh mẽ và không bị ảnh hưởng bởi bất cứ điều gì. Rồi tin tức về việc tiếp nhận Chúa và đi nhà thờ Tin lành của tôi đã đến tai của bố tôi tại quê nhà, ông đã tìm cách liên lạc với tôi và đề nghị tôi hãy về nhà gấp. Nhận được tin nhắn từ một người quen, tôi hiểu rằng một vấn đề lớn sắp xảy ra đối với tôi.

Quả đúng như vậy, khi tôi trở về quê theo như đề nghị của bố tôi và tôi gặp ngay bố tôi trước nhất. Tôi nhìn trên gương mặt ông toát lên một sự giận dữ khủng khiếp. Bố tôi không nói gì, chỉ cho tôi hai cái chọn lựa mà thôi. Thứ nhất là tôi phải bỏ ngay việc theo Chúa, quay trở về với gia đình; tuyên bố điều đó trước mặt ông và nếu tôi không thực hiện như lời hứa của mình thì ông không bao giờ xem tôi là một đứa con nữa. Thứ hai là tôi tiếp tục theo Chúa của tôi thì ông sẽ uống một chai thuốc độc đã để sẵn trên bàn để tôi chứng kiến cái chết của ông. Lúc đấy tôi đứng trước một tình huống mà tôi thấy không thể đưa ra một chọn lựa nào được. Tôi nhắm mắt lại vài giây và lắng nghe tiếng nói của Chúa, tôi nhận ra ngay một điều chúa mách bảo cho tôi đó là hãy trì hoãn những việc gì con chưa làm được bây giờ, Ta sẽ giúp con. Tôi chợt nghĩ ra một chọn lựa thứ ba và xin phép bố tôi cho tôi có một vài lời. Bố tôi đồng ý. Tôi khởi sự nói với bố một cách nghiêm túc rằng: thưa bố, con rất yêu thương bố và như bố thấy con đã cố gắng học hành để không phụ lòng bố như lâu nay. Kể từ khi con theo Chúa thì Chúa cũng dạy con phải hiếu kính cha mẹ của mình, và đó cũng chính là một trong 10 điều răn của Chúa. Vì vậy con sẽ không chọn lựa được cái nào ngay lúc này hết nên xin bố hãy cho con một chọn lựa thứ 2, đó là một tháng nữa con mới chọn một trong 2 chọn lựa của bố vừa đưa ra. Vì đây là một việc rất hệ trọng trong cuộc đời con nên con cần suy nghĩ kỹ. Điều này có nghĩa là sau một tháng nữa, đúng tại nơi này con sẽ đưa ra quyết định của mình là chọn một trong hai chọn lựa mà bố đã đưa ra cho con. Một điều lạ lùng là bố tôi chấp nhận đề suất này của tôi và không có một phản ứng gì khác. Tôi trở về lại trường của mình để học và cũng suy nghĩ cách để trả lời nhưng tôi vẫn không thấy một sự hướng dẫn nào từ nơi Chúa hết. Tôi băn khoăn lắm, nhưng ngày giờ đã đến nên tôi phải trở về quê hương mình đưa ra một quyết định chọn lựa của mình. Tuy nhiên, tôi vẫn có một sự bình an tuyệt đối vì tôi tin rằng Chúa sẽ hành động khi tôi gặp khó khăn không thể giải quyết được đúng như lời hứa của Ngài cách đây một tháng.

Tôi về đến nhà vào lúc trời sập tối, tôi đang thập thò không dám mạnh dạn bước vào nhà thì bố tôi bước ra mở cửa và nói rằng "con ơi hãy vào nhà đi!" Một giọng nói từ tốn và nhẹ nhàng của bố tôi làm tôi rất khó hiểu. Tôi nhìn trên bàn không có những sự bày bố để tôi phải chọn lựa như một tháng trước. Đột nhiên bố tôi đã quỳ xuống và nói với tôi rằng: "con ơi, hãy cầu nguyện cho bố theo Chúa của con." Tôi vẫn chưa hiểu điều gì xảy ra nhưng vì vui mừng quá tôi đã quỳ xuống cùng với bố tôi và cầu nguyện cho ông tiếp nhận Chúa Giê-xu làm Cứu Chúa của mình.

Sau khi cầu nguyện xong tôi lấy lại bình tĩnh và nói chuyện với bố tôi lý do ông đã thay đổi quyết định của mình. Ông cho biết rằng: "ông quyết định theo chúa của tôi vì ông quá sợ Chúa". Trong một tháng vừa rồi rất nhiều sự cố xảy ra trong gia đình của tôi làm cho bố tôi muốn ngã quỵ, nhiều lần trong 1 tháng qua ông đã nghĩ đến cái chết vì một người anh trai của tôi là hiệu trưởng của một trường học gần nhà đã ba lần muốn giết bố của tôi vì những lý do không có gì là quan trọng, ông cũng không hiểu vì sao anh trai tôi đã tỏ ra thái độ như vậy.

Chưa hết, một người em của tôi trong một tháng vừa qua đã chơi bài bạc thua sạch tiền và đã bán hết tất cả tài sản trong nhà để trả nợ. Điều này chưa bao giờ xảy ra trước đây trong gia đình tôi. Ngay trong lúc này, bố tôi so sánh với những gì tôi để lại cho gia đình mà ông cho là bỏ tổ tiên thì ông hối hận với những sự cáo buộc của mình, cũng chính lúc này, ông nghĩ ngay đến Chúa tôi đang tôn thờ có quyền năng siêu nhiên điều khiển mọi thứ đang xảy ra. Ông nghĩ đến sự trì hoãn của tôi là để cho Chúa hành động và nếu bây giờ ông tiếp tục chống lại Chúa nữa thì sự trừng phạt của Chúa sẽ không khiếp đến dường nào vì vậy ông quyết định đi theo Chúa để hy vọng Ngài tha thứ cho mình.

Kể từ khi bố tôi tin nhận Chúa, ông đã gặp sự bắt bớ tàn khốc hơn tôi rất nhiều, nó đến từ một người em trai của ông, chú của tôi, là một người đã có nhiều năm đi theo Cộng sản trước đây và bây giờ vẫn là một thành viên tích cực trong đảng Cộng sản. Khi tôi theo Chúa ông cũng đã nhiều lần cảnh báo với tôi nhưng vì tôi là cháu và đi học xa nhà nên ông không có thời gian gặp tôi được. Nhưng với bố tôi thì ông thường gặp và tất nhiên điều đầu tiên ông khuyên bố tôi là phải từ bỏ đạo ngay lập tức. Lúc này, bố tôi lại đứng trước một chọn lựa khó như tôi lúc trước đó là một bên nghe lời con để theo Chúa và một bên nghe lời người

em để bỏ Chúa. Tuy nhiên ông vẫn tin vào quyết định của tôi
nhiều hơn nên ông cũng tìm cách trì hoãn đối với chú của tôi.
Kể từ đây, tôi bắt đầu lên kế hoạch để cầu nguyện cho chú của
tôi mỗi ngày. Mỗi lần tôi và ông gặp nhau thì chú cháu vẫn vui
vẻ với nhau nhưng ông luôn luôn nhắc tôi phải bỏ không theo
Chúa nữa vì Tin lành là đạo của Mỹ. Tôi đã nhiều lần giải thích
với ông hiện tại mối quan hệ giữa Việt Nam và Mỹ đang tiến
triển rất tốt và quá khứ chiến tranh đã lùi dần vào dĩ vãng rồi.
Với lại đạo Tin lành không phải là đạo của Mỹ mà suất phát từ
Do Thái. Sau đó ba năm thì bố của tôi đã về với Chúa sau một
lần đột quỵ. Chú của tôi tiếp tục sống thêm 10 năm nữa. Trong
10 năm này mỗi năm tôi cố gắng gặp chú tôi một lần để nói Về
Chúa cho ông. Vào một ngày hè năm 2007 tôi nhận được một
cuộc điện thoại từ một người con của chú tôi, người này cho tôi
biết là chú của tôi đang nguy kịch trong bệnh viện và có lẽ sẽ
không qua khỏi nhưng ông luôn nhắc con của ông điện thoại cho
tôi nói rằng ông sắp ra đi rồi và muốn tôi có mặt để cầu nguyện
cho ông. Tuy nhiên người em này chỉ là người chuyển tin nhắn
mà thôi chứ không biết ý ông nói cầu nguyện là làm gì. Tôi nói
với người em của tôi rằng: "em không biết nhưng mà anh đã biết
bố của em muốn anh cầu nguyện cho việc gì rồi".

Tôi tin chắc rằng ông muốn tiếp nhận Chúa trước khi lìa khỏi
thế gian này. Nhưng ngay lúc đó tôi rất bận công việc của Hội
thánh nên không thể nào đi thăm chú tôi được vì nó nằm ở
miền Trung cách Sài Gòn đến cả 1000 cây số. Nhưng tôi nói với
người em của tôi rằng, em cứ yên tâm đi anh sẽ cầu nguyện và
tin chắc rằng bố của em sẽ qua khỏi bệnh trong lần này và bố
em chỉ qua đời sau khi gặp được anh mà thôi. Người em của tôi
cũng rất ngạc nhiên về điều tôi nói. Nhưng quả thực như, vậy
chú của tôi đã khỏe mạnh và trở về nhà sau lần đó trước sự ngạc
nhiên của nhiều người trong bệnh viện. Ba tháng sau tôi quyết

định đi ra đi gặp chú tôi và cầu nguyện cho ông. Trên đường đi
tôi tiếp tục nhận một cuộc điện thoại nữa từ người em của tôi
và nói rằng hôm đấy chú của tôi đã bệnh nặng trở lại và được
đưa vào bệnh viện nên đề nghị tôi phải ra gặp ông gấp. Tôi nói,
anh đang trên đường đi ra và sẽ đến vào đêm hôm đó. Tối hôm
đó tôi đã đến nơi nhưng vì quá trễ để vào thăm ông trong bệnh
viện vì vậy tôi đã nghỉ tại một khách sạn ở gần nhà của chú tôi.
Đến 03.00 sáng hôm sau tôi nhận được một cuộc điện thoại nữa
từ người em chúng tôi, cậu ta cho biết chú tôi đã được đưa về
nhà vì gia đình muốn ông ra đi tại nhà nên bệnh viện đã cho
mang bình oxy cho ông về đến nhà. Tôi tức tốc đi qua nhà của
ông và khi vào nhà tôi thấy mọi người khóc lóc vì thấy ông nằm
hôn mê như đã chết rồi. Khi tôi bước vào thì người con trai của
chú tôi đã đánh thức ông và nói lớn vào tai ông "Anh Thanh
đã đến". Một điều lạ lùng mà mọi người nhìn thấy đó là ông đã
mở mắt ra và nhìn tôi một cách chăm chú. Tôi quỳ xuống ngay
giường của ông và nói với ông rằng, "tôi nghĩ tôi sẽ không còn
nhiều thời gian để giải thích cho chú nữa nhưng tôi tin chắc chú
đã hiểu tất cả rồi và bây giờ hãy nói theo tôi để tôi cầu nguyện
cho ông tiếp nhận Chúa." Tôi cầu nguyện cho ông và ông đã nói
theo những lời của tôi một cách rất rõ ràng làm mọi người xung
quanh rất ngạc nhiên. Sau khi cầu nguyện xong tôi nói với ông
rằng, "bây giờhú hãy im lặng để tôi cầu nguyện cho chú đi về
thiên đàng với Chúa. Sau lời cầu nguyện của tôi hai phút thì
ông đã chính thức ra đi khỏi thế gian này và tôi tin chắc ông
đang ở thiên đàng với Chúa trong lúc này.

Những năm học trong trường y khoa là những năm tôi tham
gia rất nhiều hoạt động xã hội của Hội thánh để đến với người
nghèo. Tôi đã dẫn dắt nhiều đoàn bác sĩ đi đến khám bệnh cho
những vùng nghèo, lên đến hàng 100 chuyến đi như vậy trong
nhiều năm. Đến khi ra trường vào năm 1996, Tôi phân vân phải

đi về quê hương để làm việc hoặc là ở lại Sài Gòn để có cơ hội hầu việc Chúa tốt hơn. Tôi quyết định ở lại Sài Gòn để làm việc cho một mục vụ y tế của Hàn Quốc tại Sài Gòn sau đó bốn năm tôi quyết định chuyển sang làm việc cho World Vision. Công việc ở đây rất tốt, tôi được thăng tiến trong công việc rất nhiều nhưng tôi vẫn không thấy thỏa lòng vì đây là một tổ chức cơ đốc rất lớn nhưng luôn bị theo dõi chặt chẽ bởi chính quyền nên tôi cảm thấy rất ngột ngạt và thiếu đi sự tự do. Từ đó tôi suy nghĩ mình phải cần làm một gì đó khác hơn và tôi quyết định tìm kiếm một học bổng để đi học thần học. Cơ duyên đã đến với tôi và tôi đã nhận được một học bổng cao học thần học để đi học tại Mỹ. Sau ba năm học và thực tập tôi cảm ơn Chúa và luôn đặt câu hỏi vì sao chúa lại để cho tôi đến thực tập tại một mục vụ rất khác biệt đó là mục vụ truyền giáo cho người nghiện ở trong tù tại Yakima, Washington. Thời gian thực tập tại đây tôi bắt đầu quan tâm đến người nghiện ma túy. Người lãnh đạo ở đây muốn tôi ở lại để giúp họ lâu dài nhưng tôi trả lời dứt khoát là tôi phải về Việt Nam vì Chúa kêu gọi tôi ra đi để giúp cho người Việt Nam ở quê nhà. Tôi quay trở lại Việt Nam và được hội thánh Tin lành Việt Nam miền Nam đón nhận để làm việc cho họ trong trụ sở chính của Tổng Hội tại Sài Gòn. Tôi bắt đầu gây dựng lên một ủy ban mới đó là Ủy Ban Y Tế Xã Hội để bắt đầu giúp cho Hội thánh vương ra cộng đồng một cách công khai và chính thức. Trước đây chúng tôi cũng từng làm nhưng chỉ làm việc trong "bóng tối và không công khai" với chính quyền. Bây giờ chúng tôi đã quyết định bước ra ngoài ánh sáng để làm việc này và đây là một bước tiến rất lớn của hội thánh tại Việt Nam. Chúng tôi đã làm rất nhiều dự án cho cộng đồng và giúp cho hội thánh địa phương có một ảnh hưởng rất lớn đối với cộng đồng để qua đó danh Chúa được vinh hiển. Một việc rất lớn mà tôi đã làm đó là tôi đã thành lập một đoàn y tế khoảng trên 100 bác sĩ Tin lành chuyên đi làm Medical Mission cho các vùng nghèo, chúng tôi đã tiếp cận với rất nhiều bệnh nhân ở mọi miền đất nước. Tuy nhiên, có một điều tôi luôn trăn trở đó là chúng tôi chỉ tiếp cận để điều trị cho bệnh nhân các bệnh thông thường nhưng không được phép tư vấn và tiếp chuyện với bệnh nhân vì họ sợ chúng tôi truyền giáo. Vì vậy tôi cầu nguyện với Chúa là Ngài hãy giúp cho tôi được quyền để tiếp cận với bệnh nhân tư vấn đầy đủ cho họ. Và tôi nhận ra rằng để làm được việc này chỉ khi nào tôi được phép nằm ở trong bệnh viện là người của bệnh viện thì mới làm được. Nhưng khổ thay nếu tôi là nhân viên của bệnh viện thì lại bị quản lý chặt chẽ cũng không có cơ hội để nói về Chúa hoặc tư vấn cho bệnh nhân một cách toàn diện. Tôi tiếp tục cầu nguyện Chúa giúp cho tôi một giải pháp vì tôi đã làm việc được 10 năm trong Hội thánh Tin lành Việt Nam miền Nam rồi. Ngay lập tức chúa đã trả lời cho tôi bằng sự kết nối với tổ chức Cure International. Tôi biết đây là ý của Chúa và tôi đã chấp nhận để làm việc cho tổ chức này. Đây là một tổ chức chuyên sâu về phẫu thuật ngoại thần kinh cho trẻ em bị não úng thủy (Hydrocephalus) và thoát vì mang não tủy (Spina Bifida). Chúng tôi đã có một Bản Ghi Nhớ với các bệnh viện đúng như những gì tôi mong muốn đó là chúng tôi hỗ trợ cho bệnh viện đào tạo bác sĩ chuyên phẫu thuật nội soi (tại Uganda) cho hai bệnh này và hỗ trợ cho bệnh viện trang thiết bị phẫu thuật, ngược lại họ cho phép chúng tôi được đặt người vào trong bệnh viện để tư vấn cho bệnh nhân một cách toàn diện và đây là cơ hội cho những bệnh nhân của chúng tôi thấy được tình thương của Chúa qua công việc của chúng tôi. Hiện tại, tôi đã làm việc với 3 bệnh viện nhi lớn nhất tại Việt Nam đó là tại Sài Gòn, Đà Nẵng và Hà Nội. Ngoài ra tôi còn chịu trach nhiệm quản lý nhiều bệnh viện khác tại châu Á nữa.

Tôi nhìn thấy Chúa đáp ứng cho tôi gấp đôi những gì tôi cầu xin, đó là công việc tại bệnh viện tại Hà nội nơi tôi có cơ hội chia sẻ về Chúa cho rất nhiều bệnh nhân và đang kết hợp với các Hội thánh địa phương để mở các Hội thánh mới. Tôi luôn luôn hỏi Chúa câu hỏi của tôi từ lúc trở về Việt Nam vào năm 2006, là "vì sao Chúa đưa tôi đi thực tập trong một mục vụ cai nghiện ma túy?" Tôi tìm đến mục vụ cai nghiện ma túy tại Việt Nam ngay năm 2016, một cánh cửa rất rộng lớn đã mở ra cho chính mình tôi và tôi đã dự phần vào đây để giúp cho các trung tâm cai nghiện tại Việt Nam từ 2016 cho đến nay. Cảm ơn chúa mỗi ngày chúng tôi hoàn thiện hơn về công tác quản lý tổ chức của mục vụ này. Và cho đến hôm nay nhà nước Việt Nam, mặc dù cố tình muốn từ chối và không chấp nhận công việc làm này của Hội thánh, nhìn thấy là sự thành công của chúng tôi không thể nào phải im lặng nữa cho nên họ đã đến tìm gặp chúng tôi và đã thảo luận về việc xem xét để cung cấp giấy phép cho chúng tôi hoạt động một cách chính thức tên toàn bộ lãnh thổ Việt Nam.

CHAPTER FIVE

Bob Smoker

I met Bob about 20 years ago when my wife Brenda and I were praying about church planting. I met with Bob to discuss the good and the bad, he had returned from Island Pond Vermont after such an effort a few years prior. More recently Bob and Jean started attending our church, Community Cornerstone Church in York. Bob would speak at various churches sharing his Vietnam ministry and he created lots of interest at our church as well. Gary Zimmerman, Ed Klinedinst, Steve Pappas and I have all joined Bob on numerous trips to Vietnam over the years. I went in 2018, aside from the heat, I really enjoyed the country, the openness of the people to want to meet and talk about their country. Most important to me, I felt safe and welcome in this Communist country. I hope to be able to return one day soon. Here is Bob's story.

From Ground Pounder to Seed Planter

I was born in York, PA, and that is where I lived most of my life. I was known as Bob, Bobby, Smoke, and Robert (when in trouble). I fondly remember standing on the corner as a crossing guard in elementary school, playing with toy soldiers, building model cars among many other things. Life was simple. We lived on East Philadelphia Street and there was a body shop in our block. All the guys within two or three blocks hung out there. Most of us even worked odd jobs there at one time or another. Things like sanding cars, cleaning shop windows, sweeping the floors, organizing paint cans and so on. One summer Bud, the owner, bought an old one room schoolhouse outside of Wrightsville and we helped him tear it down so he could build a new house. Down the hill from the schoolhouse was a stream with a dam in it. It was our swimming hole from then on...even after Bud finished his house. We spent many hours having fun there. I played drums in elementary and junior high school, and football in junior and senior school. In high school, York High, I entered the machine shop program. York Area Vocational Technical School was started after my 10th grade and I was automatically enrolled in it for 11th and 12th grade. In 11th and 12th grade I went to school two weeks and worked in industry two weeks. After high school GTE Sylvania gave me a scholarship to study Tool & Die Technology at Williamsport Area Community College, but it was the same as I had at Vo-Tech so Sylvania agreed that I should just begin my apprenticeship instead of continuing the second year. Because I had a student deferment from the draft, I could not get a deferment as the other apprentices did. As a result, I was drafted in May 1969, sent to Ft Dix NJ for basic training, and after that out west to Ft Lewis Washington for infantry school. I was drafted in mid-May and in Vietnam in early October.

Introduction to Vietnam

It was September 1969 when I graduated from Infantry school, I was 19 years old and was sent to Vietnam. After arriving in Vietnam, I was assigned to the 101st Airborne Div and sent to SERTS (Screaming Eagle Replacement Training School) located near Saigon. After SERTS, along with a bunch of other guys, I boarded a C 130 and flew north to Camp Evans where I was assigned to C 2/506 Infantry. Most of the year was spent in the dense jungle mountains west of Hue. It was a difficult life – carrying everything we owned, sleeping under a poncho, being wet almost all the time from sweat or rain, hiking the mountains almost every day, drinking water from streams or rainwater caught on the poncho overnight, wearing the same cloths for weeks on end etc. That is the life of a ground pounder – but it had two major benefits 1) there were no villages around which meant I was kept from all the social ills of the war that haunt many vets today, 2) if we saw any Vietnamese, we knew it was the enemy. Most of my combat was related to Fire Support Base Ripcord. (Information about Ripcord can be found at https://www.ripcordassociation.com/.) I returned to the US and finished my service at Hunter Army Airfield in Savanna, GA getting out of the Army in May 1971.

Introduction to Jean Adcock

While stationed at Hunter a childhood friend introduced me to a girl who was one of his coworkers – Bette Jean Adcock. We dated through the mail and when I was able to go home, we dated in person. We were married February 19, 1972.

Introduction to Jesus Christ

Jean was living at the YWCA when I got out of the Army and then moved to an apartment in Hallam. One day when I stopped to pick her up she was playing music on her record player while getting ready to go out. I sat and listened closely having never heard anything like it. It was not the music, but the lyrics. It was *Christian* music, and it was intriguing. Sometime later she invited me to go to church with her. Around that time Carl, the man I was apprenticed to at work, began telling me about the Bible and encouraged me to read the Gospel of John. I am not sure how it all transpired, but everything began to mesh... Church, Sunday School, the Gospel of John, and the things Carl was telling me. Prior to this I thought I was a Christian and these new things brought me to the realization that I had been misled all my life. I thought I would die and stand before God and my good deeds would be weighed against my bad and I would pass and be admitted to heaven because I was a good guy. Well, what I was learning from Carl, the Gospel of John, and Jean's church and Sunday School convinced me that I never really was a Christian. The first Scripture that caught my attention was John 3:16, "For God so loved the world that he gave his one and only Son, that whoever believes in him shall not perish but have eternal life." Carl told me I could put my name there in place of "world" ... God so loved *Bob Smoker* that he gave his one and only Son that *if Bob would* believe in him *Bob would* not perish but have eternal life. Carl also told me that this eternal life was a gift from God, and I could not do anything to earn it. He told me about Eph. 2:8-9, "For it is by grace you have been saved, through faith—and this is not from yourselves, it is the gift of God— not by works, so that no one can boast."

December 5, 1971, I went forward in church and accepted Jesus Christ as my savior and I was assured of the forgiveness of sins and the promise of new life with him now and in heaven after I die. My life changed.

Now looking back, I realize my life had changed *because of Jean!* It all started with that music she was playing when I went to her apartment. I do not know what my life would be now if I had not met her, but I am sure it would be empty and dreary.

Preparation for ministry

From that moment on I began to see my whole life differently and gradually learned that God was using every experience of life to prepare me for the service he planned. The Ephesian passage quoted above (2:8-9), and other Scripture, states that I was not saved by works. But the next verse does say that works are part of the deal, "For we are God's handiwork, created in Christ Jesus to do good works, which God prepared in advance for us to do." Another translation says, "we are God's *masterpiece*". God is the creator of the universe and he says I (and all who believe in him) am his masterpiece. I have been to some spectacular places and seen many magnificent scenes in print and digitally, but God says *I* am his masterpiece! It is not because of what I have made of myself, but because of what he is making of me.

So I started to read and study the Bible and listening to preachers on the radio. In 1975 I began studying at Lancaster Bible College. I had finished my apprenticeship the year earlier. After some years of part-time studies, I realized that if I went to school full-time, I could earn a degree. Miraculously GTE

Sylvania allowed me to work part-time during the school year and full-time in the summer. Six years later I graduated with a major in Bible and a minor in Pastoral Studies...and four children. In the Fall of 1982, all six of us moved to Warsaw, IN so I could attend Grace Theological Seminary in Winona Lake. Classes went well but it was a struggle financially. I could only work part-time and our house in York did not sell. No one even looked at it the whole year we were at seminary. So, I completed the first year and then we returned to York, and I returned to working as a Toolmaker. Jean and I were spiritually defeated thinking we had followed God's leading to seminary, but it did not turn out as expected.

In 1985 we had healed spiritually and sensed God's call to pastoral ministry. We moved to Stowe, VT where I served as pastor of the Mansfield Grace Brethren Church, a Home Missions church. The first year there I worked full-time as a Toolmaker and pastoral ministry. Ministry was good, but it was not keeping pace with the prescribed growth expected by our Home Missions organization. After two years it was decided to close the church. We moved back to York and I returned to work as a Toolmaker. Both of us were extremely devastated! That is it for ministry. We are done!

Seven years later, 1994, I got involved with Grace Brethren Boys (GBB). A boys' ministry that uses outdoor skills - camping, canoeing, shooting, rappelling, map and compass skills, etc. to help boys and men grow in relationship with God. I taught rappelling and map and compass reading. Then I became GBB National Chaplain. I loved that ministry.

In the late 1990s I enrolled in Lancaster Bible College Graduate School and graduated with an MA in Bible with a Systematic Theology emphasis. Jean and I began to think about pastoral ministry again. The first Sunday of 2000 our Pastor resigned, and the pastoral search began. In April 2001 I applied for the position and was accepted. I became the Pastor of Susquehanna Grace Brethren Church July 1, 2001 and served there till the end of June 2010. The ministry was rewarding and there were some tremendous victories, and I learned a lot, but Jean and I discovered I am not cut out to be a solo pastor. After 9 years of ministry at SGBC I resigned.

Ministry in Viet Nam

During my first year as Pastor, I received a call from Grace Brethren International Missions asking if I would be interested in joining a team to explore ministry potential in Viet Nam. As a veteran combat infantryman going back to that place *never* crossed my mind. However, the more I thought about it the more excited I became. So, in January 2002 I was part of that team and on my way to Viet Nam. The experience was revolutionary! God had planted in me a love for Viet Nam and for the people. The next year Jean went along and then the year after that she went as part of the team without me. We were hooked. We did not know where all this was going, but we went through the doors as God opened them.

Earlier I referred to Ephesians 2:10, "For we are God's handiwork, created in Christ Jesus to do good works, which God prepared in advance for us to do." I believe that all Christians accomplish significant things for the Lord. I also believe that many of those things are done just in the course of everyday life as a Christian walks with the Lord and they are not even aware they are doing something God has planned and prepared them to do. Back to Carl, my Toolmaker journeyman. He saw his ministry consisting of two main things...collecting communion cups after church and repairing Volkswagens for Christian School teachers. However, he worked for the Lord every day by being an excellent Toolmaker and a reliable employee. In the process he was a good example of what a Christian should be. His life and words led at least three of us to the Lord and planted Gospel seed in everyone else.

God uses all our experiences – good and bad – for our training, benefit, the benefit of others, and his glory. "Now may the God of peace, who through the blood of the eternal covenant brought back from the dead our Lord Jesus, that great Shepherd of the sheep, *equip you with everything good for doing his will, and may he work in us what is pleasing to him*, through Jesus Christ, to whom be glory for ever and ever. Amen." (Hebrews 13:20-21) This is such an important concept, important truth! Everything that comes our way is used to equip us for the work to which he calls us.

There is another big part of our preparation for ministry in Viet Nam. Without going into any of the details, 2007 began an almost two-year series of intense family tragedies. This helped prepare us to work in a Buddhist culture, where the dominant religion is built on a failed attempt to answer the problem of pain and suffering in the world. I became clearer in my understanding of the Biblical answer and that helps me understand and work with Buddhists.

FLC

Our efforts in Tra Vinh, Viet Nam began in 2002. There were too many valuable interactions with many different people to tell here, but the most significant door opening was in March of 2011 when I discovered the Foreign Language Center (FLC) and was invited to teach a conversational English class the next year. So, Jean and I made plans for a 3 month long stay and arrived in Tra Vinh toward the end of February 2012. I started to work at the FLC right away. It was important to be open about who I was right from the start. So, I told the FLC officials, "I am a Christian and I love God and I love people and want to help others do the same. The best way for me to do good for the people of Tra Vinh is to help with English education. If I do good things for the people of Tra Vinh maybe they will think well of my God. I understand the role of boundaries and will not use my position as teacher to push my beliefs on anyone, but if asked a question I will answer." Later I told the FLC lead teacher, Ms. Thanh Thuy, and the Department of Education and Training English Specialist, Ms. Phuong Thuy, that I had served in the US Army in Viet Nam during the war. This openness allowed us to work in Tra Vinh without being afraid we would be "found out" and it gave us a very real sense of freedom.

I taught a Communicative English class along with a Vietnamese assistant, Ms. Vo Tran Bao Thu. The success of the class proved to the administration of the FLC the value of having foreigners work at their school. The lead teacher told me, "Whether it is only one day or one hour your time is valuable to us and we are happy to have you and your friends." It was shaping up to be a very good relationship. We were also free to discuss spiritual subjects as they came up in class. During one of the classes in 2013 one of the American helpers was asked in class about ghosts. She gave a brief answer and then asked the teacher how much she could say. The teacher told her to say as much as she wanted on the subject. That happened several times.

In March I facilitated (with a great deal of help from two American friends working in English education in Hanoi) English workshops for the province's primary school English teachers, about 180 teachers in all.

After the workshop success I proposed a summer 2013 English project to Phuong Thuy to help her teachers. The proposal was accepted by the Department of Education and Training.

SCM

I met Nhan the first day of class at the FLC. He and his wife, Chanh Da, sold sugar cane drink on the corner next to the FLC. He wanted to practice English, so I always visited them on the way to school and on the way home. I even helped with the sugar cane prep. It was great fun, and we became good friends and were having some good spiritual conversations. I had many questions about Buddhism and knew it could be a good bridge to sharing the Gospel. Since he had been a monk and was also teaching Khmer history and culture, I trusted his answers. Nhan took me to several Buddhist pagodas and gave me a book en-titled How to Practice Buddha's Teachings & The Aim Of Life.

Nhan was beginning to see real Christianity. He was seeing it lived out in the Americans who came at great expense to vol-unteer at the FLC. He was seeing that these Westerners were different from others he had seen. One day in late June there was festival at one of the pagodas in Tra Vinh city. Dem Thu (an English teacher at the FLC who a very aggressive Buddhist is "evangelist") invited some team members from the California team to go. Nhan and Chanh Da also went, and what they observed must have made a significant impression. Dem Thu began to press the Californians to worship the sun. "It is a moment that will not come again for a long time so you must worship the sun now." They answered steadfastly that they are Christians and only worship the true and living God. She insisted strenuously and they resisted and finally walked away from her. As they turned to walk home, they saw that Nhan and Chanh Da had witnessed the whole thing and their look indicated that they were embarrassed by Dem Thu's aggression but impressed with the response of the Christians.

Early in July Nhan went to Cambodia for a week to visit his brother, a long-time Buddhist monk. When he came back, he said to me, "I want to go to church with you." This was the same week that my TEL colleague in Ho Chi Minh City, Robbie McNerney, came to help with the English clubs. Robbie had been in Viet Nam for several years and had done formal language study in country. His Vietnamese ability is excellent. As is true of all our American associates who came to Tra Vinh he met Nhan and Chanh Da. However, he connected with them in a much deeper way due to his language ability. He also gave Nhan a Vietnamese Gospel of Mark. That was on a Friday.

Saturday night I went to his sugar cane corner to ask if he wanted to go to church the next day. He said he could not because he had a prior obligation. I noticed there was something different about him, he looked troubled. So I asked him about it. "I read the book Robbie gave me. How Jesus died and came back to life. I now believe God." The following Sunday he and Chanh Da went to church with me. They were warmly welcomed and felt very comfortable. They even saw other Khmer people in the congregation. It was now mid-July, and I was meeting with him in his home every day. We had wonderful conversations about spiritual truth. One day he asked what "bap-tem" means. So that day we talked a lot about baptism...its meaning and purpose, why a person is baptized and that it does not give salvation, and so on. The very next Sunday the entire church service was about baptism and there were 13 people baptized. After church he said to me, "Now I understand clear." On another occasion we talked about the truthfulness and inspiration of the Scriptures. At one point I said that people in North America, Europe, Africa, Asia, and South America all read the same inspired words of God. It is in writing, not passed along by oral tradition and therefore unchanging for the whole world. His reply – "It's the only constant."

Over the couple weeks we had together between his coming to faith in Jesus Christ and my return to the US we talked about many subjects. Sometimes after discussing a subject one day he would bring it up again the next day coming at it from a different angle from the day before and he was right on. His grasp of spiritual truth was very encouraging. The last day I visited in his home he asked me about the maps in the back of the Bible. So, we talked about Paul's missionary journeys and how God sent him to all those places to tell people the Gospel. When I was leaving his house that day, he pointed to the world map on his wall. He put his finger on the map and drew an imaginary line as he said, "God sent you from Pennsylvania to Tra Vinh so I could know God."

He told me, "I learn about God in English from you and in Vietnamese from Pastor Dien and teach my wife in Khmer." He wants to tell everyone, and he is an outspoken witness. He said if they do not want to listen it's OK and he doesn't push it... unlike Dem Thu. Pastor Dien saw that potential and has been preparing him to reach other Khmer people. In July 2014 he and Chanh Da were baptized.

Ministry during COVID-19

Over the years since 2013 we have attempted to help Nhan grow in his faith. Prior to COVID several of us were doing this in person. Nhan and I also connected by Face Book Messenger. Since COVID that has become our only way to connect. Our regular "visits" have developed into something more...a group Bible Study. Now there are four Americans and one Cambodian meeting with Nhan on a weekly basis discussing the Bible. Praise God!

CHAPTER SIX

Scott Hower

I met Scott when our mutual friend George brought him to the CR group in Columbia. As time went on, Scott and I started meeting several times a month for breakfast and I encouraged him to consider reading the Bible daily. At this time, all our leaders were expected to do the same and we used the Daily Bread as a guide to read, The Bible in a Year. This kept us mutually accountable as we were reading the same scripture daily. I really began to enjoy Scott and witness the Lord changing his life. Eventually we invited Scott and his wife Deb to join our leader team. Our CR group ran until May 2016 and soon Scott was starting a CR group at the Biker Church in York. While in Columbia he led our worship time and occasionally brought a few friends to provide live music. Scott has become a brother and friend, here is his story:

I am Scott a believer and follower of Jesus Christ and I have struggled with alcohol and sex addiction in the past.

I was born in Columbia, Pa and have a younger sister, I attended church as a child but stopped going by the age of 7 or 8.

My mom was a Sunday school teacher, but my Dad never went. Alcohol has always been a part of my family as far back as I can remember, I have pictures of me as a young child with a beer bottle in my hand. I spent a lot of time in bar rooms as a kid, with my parents and grandparents. I remember sitting there drinking Shirley temples. Think these things shaped me at an early age. I thought drinking was what everyone did, I started drinking at the age of 11. Remember drinking out of bottles from my parent's liquor cabinet and walking to school drunk.

Mom and dad were always working, and it was easy to get away with. I was always the chubby kid in school and never felt like I fit in, and never felt like I was good enough at home either. Always told by my dad how bad I did things, even had to quit the Little League team he coached because he would use me as an example of what not to do, that's still something my family thinks is a joke, but it really isn't. I was 10 or 11 when I discovered stacks of porn magazines and movies in my dad's closet, this formed the way I viewed women at a young age and thought that's how you showed love thru sex. At the age of 13 I started having sex. At that same age I started getting serious about music and soon spent all my time isolated in my bedroom for hours, sometimes 8 hours a day playing guitar. Also felt like this was the only way I could get the attention I was starving for.

Skip ahead a little bit to junior high, I drank more every weekend and smoking pot once and awhile, couple of failed relationships, had a steady girlfriend in high school who I found out cheated on me right before senior prom which destroyed me, and from that time on told myself that would never happen again, and made sure I would be the one cheating and never put myself in that position again.

I played drums in the high school marching band which introduced me to a whole new crowd, we would party together all the time. I had relationships with numerous girls in the band and band front, never having a relationship with God, pretty much living my life without a care.

I joined a popular local band at the age of 19 and we were playing bars right away and my drinking really took off. It was a way to meet more women who were interested in the bad boy musician, the more I drank the worse decisions I made. We were like a gang, getting into fights, drinking like crazy, getting barred from clubs and some barred me for life. At that time, I was also being trained in martial arts for all the wrong reasons, just a tip that alcohol and karate do not go together. The band was offered a record deal with Sony records which we blew because of drugs and alcohol in the band. I always struggled with my weight and was very self-conscious. When playing in bands in the late 80s and early 90s you had to be stick thin and have long hair. I really got into taking speed to lose weight and got down to 128 pounds with all my clothes on, taking laxatives and anything I could to drop weight. At the age of 19 I met a girl and at the age of 22 we had a baby girl together. I thought this would fill a void in my heart, but it did not, I was cheating on my girlfriend with numerous women and never really cared about any of them, but told them all I loved them, which I used to get what I wanted from women. I had a love and relationship addiction and felt like I needed someone to make me feel loved and needed. When I did not feel loved, I would start another relationship, never ending the ones I was already in.

Around this time my sister was raped by three of my best friends, and when that happened, my brother-in-law and I went after them. I was arrested for assault with a deadly weapon because of using a club on one of them. When it came down to it, the guy would not testify against me because someone talked to him about it and charges were changed to disorderly conduct.

Then on September 11th, 1991 my whole life was changed forever! My grandfather owned a car lot in Columbia and was taking some customers for a test drive and they beat him to death and ran over him with the car they stole. This affected me badly as I was the last one to see him alive. I was at the car lot because my band practiced there, it was after hours and he told me some people wanted to take a test ride. I told him not to and to tell them to come back the next day, but he was all about making the sale. I said ok and the band and I packed up and went out for a night of partying. I got a call about 1 or so saying he never came back so my brother-in-law and I got some guns and went into Lancaster city, looking for them and the car. We did not find them, or I would be the one in jail and I was called into the police station because I saw them. They were captured in New York still driving the car with a dealer plate on it. They were sentenced to jail for life with no chance of parole. This really made my drinking worse, I felt responsible for not stopping him from going on that test drive. One night soon after that I spent all night drinking and after attending an afterhours club, I made my way home to Lancaster. I was unable to keep my car in my lane the whole way home and made it within a mile or so from my house when I passed out around a corner and hit a car head on. I jumped out and flipped out on the other guy, telling him he crossed into my lane, I think he believed it as he was on his way to work at 6 in the morning. The police showed up and the lady cop said you smell like you have been drinking, I said give me a breathalyzer if you want, she said no, you are not stumbling around, that was close.

Soon after that my first daughter's mother and I parted ways; my daughter was two years old. Shortly after that I met the love of my life Deb. After a long day and night at a recording studio the band decided to stop at a club we often visited. There she was, our bass player happened to know her and introduced us, and right away I knew there was something different about her. She was 6 months pregnant, that was different...we talked for a long time, and it was cool because I never felt like talking to other girls I knew. Shortly after we started dating, she had a son who I consider my son because I've been with him since birth. He was born on my birthday two months premature which was tough, she had to spend 3 weeks in the hospital and Alex had to remain in the NICU for a while. We did a lot of partying with her sister and our friends and I played in a couple different bands at this time. And then I asked Deb to marry me and she said she would if I promised not to move off to California with the band to try to get famous and I agreed, later I would use that as a resentment. We were married June 29th, 1996.

In April of 1997, our beautiful daughter Allison was born, and I was just blown away by the miracle of her. I decided I was going to stop playing for a while so I could spend more time at home. That lasted two years, I got into a band that was only playing like once a month, I thought that would be ok. Wow these guys were a bunch of drinkers and that triggered my drinking and it got much worse and I would get drunk every time. We soon started attending church at our pastor's house and helped with his church plant. We really enjoyed it and it was growing and we were getting very involved. I never really knew we needed a relationship with Jesus. I played in the worship band at church and was coming most Sunday's hungover. I eventually started my own business, and it went well for a while till the economy took a downturn and so did the business. I felt depression setting in and was at a place where I felt something was missing. Searching online I started seeking things, starting with porn which turned into meeting women from sites and this put me in a downward spiral of despair and hopelessness. I wanted to stop but I could not and did not understand what was going on. I loved my wife but could not stop my behavior. I knew it would ruin everything I have ever wanted, a wonderful, beautiful family, but my addictions and Satan were winning!

I joined another band which really fueled my ego, my wife did not want me to be in two bands, but I told her if she did not agree I was leaving her, so she agreed. I really used this as an opportunity to drink more and have affairs, she trusted me and never thought I could do the things I was doing. But she found out and confronted me and I denied everything! The trust was broken, and she no longer believed a thing I said, I agreed to go to counselling. I was not cooperating and continuing my bad behavior. The counselor eventually told us we were wasting our money because I did not really want to work on our marriage, he was right, I did not. I thought I wanted to live my Rockstar life I had missed out on, so the day after our 15-year anniversary we separated. I told her we would get back together, but I did not think that would happen. After a few more acts of bad behavior on my part she told me, do not text, do not call, and do not come see me. That was tough even though I deserved it, I never thought it would happen. Deb was becoming stronger and little did I realize God was working on her in a mighty way.

I was living in a room at my cousin's apartment becoming more depressed. I remembered Deb telling me that exercising helps so I started walking the Wrightsville bridge every morning before work This was not always a good idea because I would look over the edge and think about jumping onto the concrete not the water. I thought everyone would be better off without me, my business was failing, marriage was failing, and I felt hopeless, I thank God that the day I considering jumping, I got a call and was offered a job. This was perfect timing and could only be God because Deb was no longer supporting me, and I really needed to work. About that time, Deb's sister gave her a pamphlet from Celebrate Recovery to pass along to me. She had been going and God had been making great changes in her life and she thought it would be good for me to check it out. Well, in August of 2011, I started attending CR at LCBC on Monday nights. The first night I was there, I wept during all the worship songs and small group. I was totally broken. I met George the first night I was there, and he really made an impact on me and I knew he had something special... it was Jesus and I wanted that.

I continued drinking for about a month and still wasn't born again. Soon after, I started attending CR in Columbia and Men's Frat and went back to the Christian counselor that Deb and I had gone to. This time I went by myself and started opening and being honest with him and myself and others. Deb and I started talking more and one day she told me she was not listening to any more secular music, which I thought was crazy because I did not think there was any good Christian music. That day I turned on WJ TL and heard a pastor talking about a book he had written called To Kill a Lion, which is all about killing lust at the root and they were talking about a men's transformation weekend they were having at Petra church. It sounded interesting, so I signed up, took a sleeping bag, and slept on the floor at Petra church and it was an amazing weekend. I had 100 guys praying for me and at that time I gave my life to Christ and felt an immediate change that was hard to describe. I came back after that weekend and told the guys in the band I would be quitting after our last show in September as I felt I could not do that anymore. That last show was the last time I drank, on September 30, 2011. I also told the guys in my other band that I was no longer playing bars and if they wanted to do it without me that was fine, but they decided we would just do weddings and private stuff.

Soon after that I met a guy at Columbia CR named Chris and I started to take him to LCBC on Mondays and men's frat. He invited me to attend his grandfather's men's breakfast on Wednesday mornings. He said he was a street preacher, and I did not know what to think, but they welcomed me with open arms and have been a true blessing. In October 2011 Deb and I talked and decided we were going to give our marriage the chance it deserved. we were both saved now and on the same path of growing in the Lord. It has been so exciting... we get up early every day and do devotions together and we read the entire Bible in a year through The Daily Bread, which one of the leaders recommended... Thank you, Pete. The men at the Men's breakfast were also involved in the Christian Motorcyclist's Association. Deb and I joined and really love being a part of a group of real friends who are not faking that they really care about us. Eventually we got involved in a Bible study at Jack and Majella's house and it has been a blessing being able to learn more and more about how important it is to share your faith.

I want to continue growing and learning, because when you stop growing, you are not standing still, you are going backwards. It is just so important to surround yourself with good Christian friends. Proverbs 13:20 says "He who walks with wise man will be wise, but the companion of fools will be destroyed" and

1 Corinthians 15:33 says "Do not be misled, bad company corrupts good character." I eventually quit the other band and was wondering what I was going to do. All I ever wanted was to be a musician, but I gave it to God and if I was not supposed to play anymore, I was okay with that. But He had other plans... I was asked to join the worship team at church and formed a band specifically to play at CR and had lots of other doors open like Manos House ministry where many young boys gave their hearts to the Lord. I got involved in the coffee house ministries, which has been awesome too. We are having fun playing music for the Lord and ministering to people. The Lord has blessed me over and over. He has restored my marriage, my family and blessed me with true friends that I truly love and cherish.

With God's help and direction, I have been able to forgive the people that killed my grandfather and freed myself from the guilt. He has given me the ability to remain in recovery, by being in the Word every day, praying continually and making meetings a priority. Jesus is not just a part of my life; he is my life. I am now a core team member, worship leader and Celebrate Recovery ministry leader at Freedom Biker Church. The last 10 years in recovery have been the best years of my life.

CHAPTER SEVEN

Lisa Calhoun

I met Lisa at least 10+ years ago at a Celebrate Recovery meeting in Columbia or it may have been a Christian music festival in the area. My time with her was most often while she was leading HUB or His United Body in York. This is a wonderful opportunity to share testimonies, enjoy delicious Parma Pizza and enjoy fellowship with other Christians. I also hired Lisa to list my mothers' home when she passed, and it sold in days. It was a pleasure dealing with her professionally as well as her being a Godly woman. She, her sister Deb and brother-in-law Scott have all become dear friends of Brenda and I.

Hi, my name is Lisa. I am a grateful believer & follower of Jesus Christ. On May 21st, 2011, my life completely changed. God revealed to me how alcohol had affected my life & my relationship with Him. He set me free from alcohol that day & within the next year He set me free from drugs, prescription pills & cigarettes. I also struggle with trust issues in relationships with men, codependency, fear of abandonment issues & issues with food.

I was born in Owings Mills, MD in 1970. My parents had 3
children together. My sister Deb is 2 years older than me & my
brother Dan is 4 years younger. Deb was always the rule follower & kind of like the little mother hen to us when we were
growing up (& still kind of is...Lol). My little brother Dan was
the spoiled one that got away with everything. And I was the
middle child, always kind of carefree & a little wild!

I think we had a good childhood. We did a lot of things together as a family & our parents loved us. We would go to church
sporadically (except Dad, he usually only went on Christmas &
Easter, if he went then). I know I asked Jesus into my heart as a
young child, but I was never really taught about having a relationship with Him. I believe I was saved at a young age, but I did
not become a follower of Jesus until 2011. Dad was always into
some "new hobby" so we got to experience a lot of things when
we were growing up. My Dad was in a Southern Rock band &
he also did Elvis impersonations. He looked ALOT like Elvis
in his younger years & could sing like him too! But as you can
imagine a handsome man that looked & sang like Elvis caused
a lot of trust issues in his relationship with my Mom. We had a
sailboat, so we spent a lot of weekends at Codorus Lake boat-
ing & camping. My Dad used to race motorcycles so us kids had
dirt bikes too. Then Dad got into horses, so my parents bought
a small farmette in Stewartstown. We each got our own horse
(except Mom, she was kind of scared of them). We would go
trail riding & then we began showing horses & participating in
competitions. My horses' name was Sunshine. She was a beautiful sorrel color with a blond mane & tale. I remember just loving her so much! A lot of our time was spent taking care of all
the chores around the farm. As much as I complained about
everything we had to do, I do believe that it helped us kids to

become responsible & it helped to instill a good work ethic in each of us, that we have each carried into our adult lives.

As a child I recall Mom & Dad fighting at a lot when they would go out when Dad's band played. They would usually be drinking those nights. And a lot of the women would be flirting with Dad & throwing themselves at him when he did his Elvis acts. I believe this caused a lot of insecurities for my Mom & she probably drank even more to cope with all those feelings. I believe Dad enjoyed all the attention from the women. He was always quite the flirt with all the women. Eventually my Dad was unfaithful to my mom. When Mom found out he was having an affair & that he had taken this woman up to his hunting cabin, she was done. They sat us kids down the day before Christmas in 1982 & let us know that Dad would be moving out the day after Christmas & they would be getting a divorce. I think I was in shock after Mom & Dad told us this. Even though I knew they had problems in their marriage. I just thought they would always work things out & would always be together.

So, after Dad left our lives changed A LOT! We would only see Dad on Wednesday evenings for dinner & eventually would go to spend every other weekend with him. The woman my Dad had an affair with was also 16 years younger than my Dad and she was only 7 years older than my sister. She eventually married my Dad & they had 2 children together. We have a half-brother & sister, Jimmy & Emily that are about 20 years younger than us. Eventually my Dad went through another divorce after he found out that she had an affair with another man. I believe this was a turning point for my Dad when he realized how much being unfaithful can hurt your spouse & he called my mom &

took her to breakfast & apologized to her for hurting her like that when he cheated on her.

Our home life was VERY different after Dad had left. Mom was working all the time to make ends meet. She was a Realtor, so she worked a lot of evenings & weekends, So we had a lot of un-supervised time at home. This was when Deb & I began hanging out with teenage boys & we started drinking alcohol, smoking cigarettes & smoking weed. I was 12 & she was 14. The next year I met a guy named John that I liked. He was a few years older than me & was one of those "bad boys". He quickly became my boyfriend. Before I knew it, we were having sex. I was not on the pill or using protection. The next month after we started having sex, I realized that I did not get my period & when I was walking to my bus stop in the mornings, I was feeling nauseous. I think I was in denial because I let another month pass before I said something to my mom about it. She took me to Planned Parenthood & they did a pregnancy test. They told me how far along I was & said that if I was going to have an abortion, I only had a couple of weeks left to have that done. So, I quickly made the decision that I wanted to have an abortion. I had recently heard that John had cheated on me & although he denied it, I was certain that he did. He wanted me to have the baby, but I told him I was not ready to raise a child. I was planning on going to college & had to still get through high school. The day before Thanksgiving in 1984 I aborted my baby. This was a decision I have deeply regretted & I believe I hated myself most of my life because of it. I ended my relationship with John a couple of months later.

As a result of Mom & Dad divorcing, we had to sell the farm & the horses. Mom bought a house in York, in York Suburban

School District. This was a complete culture shock for us because this school was known as "Snob Hill" where a lot of rich kids went to school & the school, we just moved from was known for being a "Hick School" with a bunch of farmers. My sister & I quickly found new party friends at our new school & continued with our party lifestyle. During this time, I started experimenting with cocaine too.

I started working at the age of 14 & when I was a senior, I had 2 part time jobs & continued to be an honor roll student all through high school. I ended up being the Homecoming Queen my senior year, which was very shocking because I was not a cheerleader or in sports or involved in any school activities. I was on the DO program (Diversified Occupation) that allowed me to go to school for a half day & go work a job for the other half. I did not have a boyfriend at that time, so I asked one of my best friends (Dan) to be my escort. He was one of the biggest pot heads in high school. He ended up getting suspended from school right before our Homecoming. So, the principal said that he could escort me to the football game, but he could not come to the homecoming dance. I had to ask another friend of mine to be my date for the dance that night. I was probably the 1st Homecoming Queen in York Suburban's history that was a party girl, in the DO program that was not involved with any school activities and that had 2 different guys escort her to the game & dance!

My intention was always to go to college after I graduated from high school, but when the time came, I did not know for sure what I wanted to go to college for. I thought that I would probably like to be a teacher (like my sister was in college for). I started the application process at York College but was quickly frustrated with filling out the financial aid paperwork. I thought if I have this much trouble filling out this paperwork, how would I ever make it through college?? I decided to take off a year after I graduated to try to figure out what I wanted to do. I began to party even more this year. Our mom had moved to Florida & let my sister & I stay in the house & we just had to pay the utilities. Our house quickly became known to be the "party house". We had friends that were dealing coke, so they would come to our house to cut it up to sell. That became plentiful & I was doing it more often. I changed my mind a few times that year as to what I wanted to do with my life. I thought about going to school to become an airline stewardess so I could travel around the world, but then decided I did not really want to live most of my life in hotels. Then I thought about becoming a hairdresser but then thought about standing on my feet all day for hours on end & that did not sound too great either. So as time crept on & I was still undecided about what I wanted to do & I was partying more & more and I started to get depressed. One night when I was closing the restaurant where I worked, my boss George who I had worked for since I was 14 asked me what was wrong with me lately. He noticed that I had not been myself. I told him that I was getting depressed because I did not know what I wanted to do with my life. He said, "You should get into real estate". I said, "Well, my mom was in real estate for 10 years before she moved to Florida, but I can't really see myself doing that because I don't think I'm really a salesperson". George said, "I see you with the people & you're good with people." I called my mom the next day to find out what would be involved with getting into real estate. When she told me that you only had to take 60 hours of classes & then pass a state exam. I thought, that is my kind of school. I signed up for the classes & within a few months I was a licensed realtor at the age of 19!

Along with my new career came lots of drinking. Some of the agents in my office liked to end their day at a local bar & grab a bite to eat together & have a few drinks. I started dating another agent at my office & this became part of our daily routine. We dated for about 2 years until the trust had been broken. I had found out that some women went with the guys to a "guys weekend" at the beach. After that I began to 2nd guess everything about him, so I ended the relationship.

I was now officially 21 & could legally go to the bars! I had been getting into bars since I was 16 or 17, but it felt good to FINALLY be able to go to whatever bars I wanted to go to!

I was now hanging out with some other single girlfriends that liked to go see bands. We traveled to Baltimore a lot to go to Hammerjacks on the weekends. I usually drove when we went out. When I look back on how many times, I was in no shape to drive, but somehow always got home safely, I realized how many times God had been protecting me over the years. For the next 4 years I partied & worked a lot as I was building my real estate career. I do recall many Sundays when I had open houses scheduled that I would be so hung over. When there were not buyers coming through the house I would doze off on a couch or if it was a vacant house, I would lay down on a bedroom floor until I heard the doorbell ring. I look back on that now & think about how obvious it was that I had a drinking problem, but back then I did not think anything about that kind of stuff.

In 1995 I met Thomas, the man that I would spend the next 14 years of my life with. Thomas was a good man, but like a lot of us, he battled addictions most of his life. He had been sober a few years before I met him, but he was no longer. He usually just drank a few beers, but he LOVED his weed! He also struggled with depression & anger issues that stemmed from his childhood. One of the things I loved about him was how loyal he was. I had not been with many men over the years that I trusted, but I did trust him. During this time in my life, I became a workaholic. I had been hired as the company recruiter for a growing Century 21 office & I was still selling homes too. In the early 2000's I was making over $200k a year in the booming real estate market. Thomas & I had bought a home together. It was a cool little geodesic dome house on 3 acres with a beautiful view of the Susquehanna River. It needed a ton of work, but Thomas was able to do a lot of the work himself. So, we knew it would work for us. We also ended up buying a couple of investment properties. And I was buying investment properties with my friend Stacey. She & I even purchased 2 condos in Myrtle Beach as vacation rental properties. My plan was that the investment properties would be my retirement plan because I had not put much money into a retirement account over the years.

At some point Thomas injured his knee & was prescribed pain medicine for it. After he had the surgery on his knee & the doctor stopped prescribing the meds, he began to get a bunch of Percocet & Xanax from one of his friends. He was also prescribed Adderall for his ADD. He let me try his Adderall because I was usually up late doing computer work & I needed a little pick me up. I quickly became hooked on them because I could get so much more done when I took them! I also started trying his Percocet & Xanax & then decided I was going to start getting my own prescriptions. I went to my doctor & told him that I was sure that I had ADD because I could not focus & I would like to try Adderall & he prescribed it to me. I then went in & told him that I was having back issues from when I bungee jumped when I was younger. he prescribed Percocet & muscle relaxers. So, between the hundreds of pills Thomas was getting from his friend plus what we both were getting through prescriptions we were both completely hooked on pills. Thomas also had a love for fireworks (or maybe it was more like an addiction). He would shoot them off whenever he wanted. The cops came to our house several times because our neighbors would call in & complain and he was warned several times it had to stop. One night while I was at work, he shot some off and he took off & went to a bar. Our neighbor called me & said the cops were at our house looking for Thomas. I called him to let him know & he said he was going to wait awhile & then he was going to back to the house & pack up all his fireworks & take them up to his parents' house in Hershey to hide them. I came home from work & he asked if he could put them in my Pathfinder so if he passed the cops on the way out, they would not know it was him. So, I said he could but while loading up he came running inside & said that a bunch of cops just pulled in! Not only was it the local police with a search warrant for our house, but also the State Police, the DEA & the ATF. They came in & cuffed us & searched our house for hours from top to bottom. They found guns, weed, bongs & bowls, grow room stuff, pills not in prescription bottles & LOTS of fireworks! Thomas begged them to not charge me with anything. He told them I worked all the time & all the stuff they found was his. They arrested him that night & charged him with risking a catastrophe, because of all the illegal fireworks & there were a bunch of other charges too, but that was the big one, because it was a felony. They did not arrest me that night, but they did say that it would be up to the District Attorney whether I would get charged too. I was a wreck, because I knew if I were charged, I would lose my Real Estate license & Real Estate was my life! Thankfully, the DA did not charge me, but Thomas did end up having to do 30 days in jail & then to rehab for another 30 days afterwards and was on probation after that. One of the rules with probation was you were not allowed to have alcohol in the house. I would hide my wine coolers & vodka in my Pathfinder & in my bedroom closet in case the probation officer stopped by for a surprise visit. Years later when I looked back on this situation, I realized how much I was living in denial about my drug & alcohol abuse.

Thomas continued to spiral out of control with his pill addiction & his depression & anger issues seemed to get worse too. In 2009 I made the decision to leave him. I went & stayed with my mom one weekend & he threatened to burn our house down with everything in it. His parents drove out to our house to check on him & try to get him calmed down & when they got there, he threw a rock at their old, restored car that was his Dad's pride & joy. He told them he was going to kill himself, so they called the police. The police came out to the house to talk to him & decided that he needed to be hospitalized. He was committed to the psych ward for 3 days. I decided that I needed to go out to the house & pack up all my stuff, which included most of the furniture, before he was released from the hospital. I rented a moving truck & a bunch of my friends helped me get everything out of there in one day. The next day I went to the hospital to let him know that I moved & there was not much left in the house. I told him that I was not coming back. It was hard because I loved Thomas. I was really concerned about him killing himself & I felt like I was deserting him at a time when he needed me, but I knew in my heart that I could not continue to live like this. I did not see anything changing & I needed to do this for my own safety & sanity. Thankfully, we had 2 dogs (Sebastian & Brutus) & they became his reason for living because he had to take care of them. We also had a lot of stuff to work through financially because of the properties we owned together & it took us a few years to get all that worked out, but we did over time.

After I left, I began going to the bars again. I had not been in the bar scene much over the years that I spent with Thomas because he was not much of a socializer like I was. My sister's husband Scott was in 2 local bands that played out at the bars. So, we were always going to watch them play. I began drinking again like I did when I was in my early 20's & meeting guys in the bars like I did back then too. On Bike Night I met a guy named Mike that was playing guitar in a band at The Wheelie Bar. We hit it off right away & started hanging out together. He liked to drink & party as much as I did! We would meet up at the bar after work sometimes every night of the week on the weeks that he did not have his kids. The weeks that he did have his kids I was over at his house almost every night. I quickly became attached to them & realized that I could love someone else's kids as if they were my own. In May of 2011 Mike ended our relationship. He said that he jumped into a relationship too quickly after him & his wife had separated & was not ready for this. I was heartbroken & completely crushed. I wanted to just go get drunk & forget about him, but every time I drank, I found that I would just get more depressed thinking about him.

A guy (Dave) that I had dated when I was a teenager had been reaching out to me around this time to let me know that he was getting into the mortgage business & wanted to get together for coffee so he could try to get some of my business. On the evening of May 19th, I was out with my friends at the bar. I got a call from my sister. She had received a call from the York City police department. They said that our Mom had been in a car accident on 83. It was a rainy night & she had hit the median & totaled her car. She had been drinking & was twice the legal limit, but thankfully she walked away from that accident without injuring herself or anyone else. That was truly a miracle. The next day I had to take her to her car so she could get all her belongings out of it. I was not in a good place emotionally that day. I was upset with her because this was her 2nd DUI & I thought she was going to have to go to jail. While I was with Mom, Dave had called me. He could tell I was upset & asked what was going on, so I told him. Then he prayed with me on the phone. I felt a peace come over me & I was able to get through the rest of my day. That evening he called to check in with me to see how I was feeling. I was sitting on my front porch drinking my wine & smoking my cigarettes. He asked if he could stop over so we could catch up. So, we sat on my front porch & talked for hours that night because we had not seen each other for over 20 years. During our conversation, I told him that I was in the worst financial position I had ever been in in my life. The condos that my friend Stacey & I had bought in Myrtle Beach were upside down & we owed more against them then what we could sell them for. But we needed to sell because the rentals were not covering the mortgage payments & we were both struggling financially since the Real Estate market had tanked in 2008. I owed back income taxes & fines of about $90k from not filing income taxes since 2008 and was getting scary letters from the IRS & I was concerned I could possibly go to jail. I still owned the real estate properties with Thomas & we had separated 2 years before that, so I still had to deal with that mess. And I owed about $30k on credit cards from using them to live off the past few years when I was not making the kind of money I had been used to making.

After sharing all this stuff with Dave about how much of a train wreck I was financially. I said, "I hope this car accident & the DUI my mom got is her wakeup call because she is an alcoholic in denial". After that, Dave started asking me questions about my drinking. Then I asked him "Do you think I have a problem with drinking?" He didn't really answer and then I said, "I never drink while I'm working. I just drink when I get home at night & I want to relax & unwind or when I want to go out with my friends to have a good time. At the end of the night, it was really bothering me that he had been questioning me about "my drinking". I asked him again, "Dave, do you really think I have a problem with drinking?" He just shrugged his shoulders and said "I don't know. Maybe you should get on your knees tonight & ask God." That's what I did that night before I went to sleep, I knelt down beside my bed & said a heartfelt prayer to God. I prayed & said "God, if drinking is a problem in my life, help me to be honest with myself & if it is, help me to quit." I really could not imagine my life not drinking, because all of my friends were drinkers & it was just what I always did to relax & have a good time! The next morning when I woke up & it was a beautiful sunny day. I had plans to go to a wine festival with my girlfriends that day, but as the morning progressed, I was not feeling up to drinking that day. (which was VERY unlike me) I had planned that day off so I could go drinking & usually when it was that nice out, I really wanted to drink. But instead, I called my girlfriends to let them know that I was not going to go, because I did not really feel like drinking that day. I think they were in shock! Then I spent the day on my back porch praying, journaling & reflecting on my life. I started thinking about how I was 12 years old when I started drinking & smoking cigarettes. Then I started thinking about other kids that I knew that were 12 years old & realized how young that was!

By the time I was 13 or 14 I was smoking weed & taking speed. Then I started to think about how almost everything I did in my life that I was ashamed of I did when I was drinking or doing drugs. I was also taking a bunch of prescription pills at the time too. I would take Adderall & pain pills to pick me up & Xanax & muscle relaxers to bring me back down. So, I was not taking them as prescribed.

God opened my eyes that day & showed me that drinking was a problem in my life. The next day Dave got me connected to a friend of his (Jane). She was in recovery & involved in AA. I called her that day & we met at an AA Meeting that week. I loved her as soon as I met her! She was funny & just real & down to earth! She had been sober for 10 years & had a joy & a peace in her that I wanted too! I started going to AA meetings several days a week & asked Jane to be my sponsor. She got me started with going through the steps. I realized as I was going through them that they were leading me into a relationship with God. And although I had asked Jesus into my heart as a child, I never really had a relationship with Him. As time went by & it was weeks & then months since I had a drink, I realized that God had answered my prayer that night that I got on my knees. He helped me to be honest with myself about my drinking & to see how it had affected my life & then He removed the desire to drink & helped me to quit!! This is when I really became in awe of God! I realized that He answered my prayer & performed a miracle in my life! I wanted to really get to know Him & what HIS plan was for my life. I started listening to Christian music all the time. I could not even listen to secular music anymore because it reminded me of my old life. I started watching evangelists on TV because I was so hungry for His word! I felt like I was understanding the bible more for the 1st time in my life.

Within a few months God led me & my sister to a Celebrate Recovery Meeting at York Christian Church behind the Galleria Mall. My sister & her husband Scott were separated at the time because he had been unfaithful to her. She needed healing from all of that & CR was for anyone with hurts, habits, or hang-ups. It wasn't just for people struggling with drugs & alcohol which I thought was really cool because a lot of times our struggles with drugs & alcohol stems from other underlying issues in our lives. The 1st time we went when I heard people introduce themselves & they started by saying "Hi my name is so & so, I am a believer & follower of Jesus Christ & I struggle with..." and they share what they are struggling with. I thought "WOW...that is powerful!" because one of the things that I struggled with when I went to AA meetings was introducing myself by saying "I'm Lisa & I'm an alcoholic" because I have always believed that our words are very powerful. And if God set me free from alcohol, then I did not want to speak that as my identity over my life. Do not get me wrong, I'm very thankful for AA. I met a lot of good people there & when I worked through the steps it helped to show me how to have a relationship with God. So, I am grateful for that! I just felt different when I went to CR. And the 1st difference I noticed was with how people introduced themselves. The identity that they were speaking over themselves was that they were a "believer & follower of Jesus Christ" & then shared what their struggles were. It just felt right in my spirit to hear that & speak that! CR also helped me to realize how many people were struggling with so many different things in life, not just drugs & alcohol. And as I continued to come every Friday, I would hear what other people were struggling with & my list began to get longer. Within 6 months my sister & I joined our 1st step study together. It was an amazing journey with some beautiful women. Through that God healed a lot of things in me & He revealed things to me that I would still need to work through. We built beautiful relationships with each other as we went through it. When you become that transparent & real with each other a special bond is created with each other.

During the step study one of my sisters had shared with me that a good friend of hers had gone to a weekend retreat called Rachel's Vineyard. It was a retreat for women that had had abortions & needed healing from that. I had recently met a friend through a small women's group I had joined at LCBC in York. She also had shared with me that she had an abortion that she needed healing from too. So, the two of us decided to go to this retreat together. It was a very difficult weekend emotionally because I had buried my feelings about this so deep within me so I wouldn't have to feel them, but they all came out that weekend. What I did realize was that I was a young 14-year-old girl making an adult decision at that time in my life. I also left that weekend feeling a peace that I would someday meet my baby in heaven. I also believe that God used me a few times over the years when some of my girlfriends got pregnant & were considering having an abortion. I was able to share with them the deep regret I had carried with me my whole life with making that decision & I believe that by sharing that with them it helped them to not abort their babies.

And although having children was always something I wanted in my life & looked forward to, it has not been part of my journey yet. I used to think that God was punishing me for aborting my baby & that was why I had not been married or had children like I had always envisioned, but I now know that is not how God works! Our God is a God of love & of forgiveness. He had forgiven me the 1st time I asked Him to. It was me who had not forgiven myself.

Before my sister & I had started going to CR @ YCC I had visited LCBC church in Manheim one Saturday evening & I picked up a pamphlet about a CR meeting that they were having there. I had only heard about CR at that time, but I felt compelled to give that pamphlet to my sister to give to Scott. He was really lost & hurting at the time. My sister had asked him to move out & since they had separated, she had stopped communicating with him. I knew that he was not at a place of doing anything to make real changes in his life at that time, but I thought if he ever was then maybe he would go check it out.

Within a few months God had gotten a hold of Scott's heart too! One day my sister had told him all she listened to anymore was the Christian radio station 90.3 because secular music just reminded her of her old life. So, he started listening to that radio station too & he "just happened" to hear a pastor from Lancaster speaking about a book he had written on the struggle he had with lust. The pastor was having a men's weekend retreat & Scott ended up getting online & signed up to go to it. He had NEVER done anything like that before! That weekend he said that a bunch of men laid hands on him & prayed for him & something changed in his heart that weekend! He still had a band job with his secular band the following weekend. He followed through on that commitment but afterwards he told the guys in the band that he was done! And he was!! He started going to CR Meetings after that. He attended one in Columbia & the one at LCBC! God led him to good godly men that would mentor him & come alongside of him on his journey!

I am crying as I am typing this just thinking about how amazing our God is! God got a hold of me, my sister & my brother-in-law all within 6 months of each other! We all 3 surrendered our lives to the Lord that year! We used to all hang out at the bars together to watch Scott play in his bands & go out drinking, BUT now we are all going to CR & serving the Lord! God reconciled Deb & Scotts marriage & eventually Scott started a Christian rock band (Ransomed Soulz) to play at CR meetings & other Christian events. A few years later Scott & my sister were asked to be part of the Leadership team at a new church that was opening in York. That church is The Freedom Biker Church & they are on the "Core Team". Scott is the worship team leader & they started a CR there on Friday nights. I have come alongside them & I am part of their leadership team at CR & I have loved being a part of what God is doing there!

Shortly after I got sober I started wondering what people did on the weekends or where they would go to socialize & hang out with other people that were sober & following God. There was not really any gathering place like that to go to. I believe God gave me a vision to have a place where people would come together to socialize, listen to Christian bands & have a bite to eat together. I kept getting more details of the vision. I saw an old brick warehouse in the city that was restored into a cafe'/coffee house that had a stage for bands & decorated with artwork from local artists. It was a place where our creative gifts can be shared with each other. After I had this vision, I was at a prophetic service at the Freedom Center in Windsor. I had a prophetic word spoken over me & he said that he saw a wheel & all these spokes going into the hub of a wheel. He said that all the spokes going into the hub of the wheel represented all the different connections that I have with people I know & this represented a large ministry that I was going to have. So shortly after that night the thought came to my mind to call the place that I saw in my vision "The HUB" & HUB stood for "His-United-Body". The HUB would be a gathering place for the Body of Christ & anyone that came there would feel the LOVE of Jesus because He was at the center of everything we are doing there.

At that time, I was doing outreach ministry in York City. Every Saturday afternoon I would meet some friends at a strip center in front of a ministry called Rapha. We would hand out bottled water to people that were walking by & ask them if they needed prayer for anything. We met & prayed with a lot of people. I also started to bring clothes that I had in boxes in my basement & would hang them out on racks so they could come by & pick out what they wanted. It was beautiful how we started to build relationships with all these people. One day the leader of this outreach ministry (Susan) had suggested to me that I should start The HUB there at Rapha. I was reluctant at 1st & told her that was not what I had seen in my vision. The vision had a big building & Rapha was in a small space in this strip center. Her response was "Well sometimes God will test us & see if we are faithful in the small things 1st before He just blesses us with everything, He has shown us in a vision." So I began The HUB there in August of 2014. I decided I would have it on the 2nd Saturday of each month from 6-8pm. I wanted to serve food there, but I was in the worst financial position I had ever been in & could not really afford to buy food to serve there. I asked my friend Beth who I had met in a small group @ LCBC that owned Parma's Pizza if she could sell me pizza at a reduced price so I could serve food there. I was hoping that serving the free food might attract some of the people that we had been praying with over those past few months to come join us. Beth said that she wanted to donate the food for The HUB & did not want me to pay for it. I was just in awe of how God was providing! My brother-in-law Scott who had started the Christian band would play there & I had invited Deborah Nell a prophetic artist that had also been doing the outreach ministry with us to paint during the worship. We had beautiful evenings of fellowship & worship together & people would get up & share testimonies of what God was doing in their lives. We had The HUB there for about a year, but a new ministry had taken over that space & they no longer wanted us to have The HUB there. I just thought we would have to stop having The HUB until God blessed me with that building I saw in my vision, but NO God had another plan. A friend of mine (Aaron) had said that he asked the pastor of his church in East York if I could have The HUB at their church & his pastor said yes. This space was bigger than the space at Rapha & more people had begun to hear about The HUB & were now coming. We continued to grow but after almost 2 years of having The HUB there that door closed & was once again concerned about whether I would be able to continue to have The HUB, BUT GOD showed up again. Someone had suggested that I ask my pastor @ 1st Assembly if I could have it in the youth sanctuary. Pastor Danny said "absolutely", we have been there ever since. God has continued to bless the ministry as it continues to grow. All these years later my friend Beth & her husband Anthony have continued to faithfully provide the pizza & salad every month since it started! They have truly been a blessing to all of us at The HUB! I am still praying & believing that God will provide the building for The HUB as we continue to grow & the vision that He has given to me will be fulfilled in His timing & in His way!

Since I surrendered my life to the Lord in 2011, He has taught me a lot. First, I learned that Celebrate Recovery is not just a road to recovery but a journey of discovery...Pastor Eric from YCC CR used to say that. And it is so true. I know that through each step study that I went through the Lord was working on different things in me each time. I have discovered things that I did not know I needed to work on.

I have learned that when we trust God with our finances that He provides. I stood on His promise from Malachi 3:10 where He says to test him with tithing & see if He will not open the windows of heaven & pour out a blessing that we cannot contain! When I was in the worst financial position, I had ever been in with owing back income taxes over $90k & over $30k in credit card debt. I had heard a sermon about tithing & decided I needed to do it. I was really scared because I didn't think I could give 10% of what I was making & still be able to pay my bills & get out of the hole I had dug, but shortly after I made the commitment to trust God with this area of my life I had to make the decision whether to pay all my bills that month with a commission check I just received or whether I should tithe 1st & pay what I could from what was left over. I decided to pay my tithe 1st & as I wrote the check out for my tithe that month, I said to God that I am trusting you to provide for me God. A week or two later I received a call from a past client & he wanted to meet me for lunch. After we ate, he handed me an envelope & said that he wanted me to wait to open it until after we left. He said that God had laid it on his heart to do this. When I got out to my truck & opened the envelope there were 10 - $100 bills in it! I just started crying & thanked God for taking care of me the way He promised He would in His word! I called my friend to let him know how much he blessed me. I told him that I had just made the decision that month to tithe but did not have enough money to pay my bills. He thanked me for letting him know that, because he said he did not know if it was really God telling him to do this or not, because he had no idea I was struggling financially & he didn't want me to think he was weird for doing this. He said that it confirmed he was hearing from God!! God showed me that when we trust HIM, He will provide! I have faithfully tithed since then and within 2.5 years I had all that credit card debt & money I owed for back taxes completely paid off!

I have learned that it is important to serve. We are all part of the Body of Christ & we all have different gifts & talents & God wants us to use them to help others. When God led me to 1st Assembly of God (now Redemption International Ministries) I served wherever God needed me...in the food ministry, the children's ministry, leading a small group & eventually as a board member.

I have learned even if we do not understand why certain things have or have not happened in our lives that we are to "trust in the Lord with all our hearts and lean not on our own understanding & in all of our ways acknowledge Him & He will direct our paths." I have not understood why I have never been married or had children when that is what I have always wanted for my life, but I have realized that I don't have to understand why it has not happened yet.... all I must do is put my trust in God & in His timing. This has not always been easy for me because I tend to put my trust in my feelings (instead of what I know in my heart God is telling me to do) & when I follow my feelings it usually leads me down the wrong path.

And although I have not had any children of my own God has blessed me with some special relationships with young women that are the ages of daughters to me. One of these is Montana, who I met when she was a teenager in the House of Hope. House of Hope is a Christian ministry to help hurting teens & their families get healing & find hope through the power of the Holy Spirit & the Word of God. Montana continued to stay in touch with me after she was out of the House of Hope & we became close over the years. She is like a daughter to me. I tell everyone that she is my spiritual daughter. She is now a single mother with 2 precious kids (Audreigh & Grayson) who are my God children. I am very thankful that they are a part of my life & I love them like they are my family.

I must also mention the most recent blessings in my life. About 6 months ago I rescued a puppy. She is my little mutt from Mississippi. (well not so "little" anymore) Her name is Sadie & she is full of so much LOVE. Her foster momma thought she might only be about 10-15lbs when she was fully grown because she was so tiny, but she is now 7 months & 34 lbs & still growing! I had a DNA test & she has ALOT of different breeds in her but the breed she has the most of is a Bluetick Coonhound. I like to say, "I got me a Coonhound". Prior to rescuing Sadie, I had been looking for a Yorkie puppy, but did not realize how expensive they were. The ones that I found were anywhere from $1500-$3000 & I could not imagine paying that much for a dog. I had given up finding one & that was when I rescued Sadie, BUT one day a friend mentioned to me that her granddaughter had just gotten a Yorkie puppy. I said "OH yeah? Do you know how much she paid for it?" And she said "Yes, she only paid $600 for it. We know a lady in West Virginia that breeds them & always sells them for $600." So, I asked for her name & number. The next morning, I prayed & asked God if getting another puppy was a crazy idea & whether I should really take on this responsibility. That afternoon I ran into a Realtor in my office that I had not seen in a while. She asked me how Sadie was doing & I said, "really good & I'm actually thinking about getting another puppy, but I don't know if that is a crazy thing to do?!?!" Her immediate response was "It's not crazy at all. I have always had 2 dogs. Dogs just do better with another dog because they are pack animals, so when you're working, they have a companion." I knew that was God's answer to my prayer from that morning. I called the breeder as soon as I left the office to see if she still had one left and she texted me a picture & said she had this little boy left. As soon as I saw his picture. I said, "I'll take him!" My niece Allison suggested that I name him Theodore & I could call him "Teddy" for short. After meeting him in person & seeing how tiny he was I knew that was what I wanted to name him, and he is our little "Teddy Bear". He steals the hearts of everyone he meets because he is so tiny & cute! I thank God every morning when I pray for bringing them to me, so I could be their Momma. They have brought so much love & joy into my life! Looking back on it, I realize that God did not bless me with a Yorkie until I had adopted Sadie, because I believe it was His plan to bring them both into my life. If I had found a Yorkie 1st, I probably would not have started searching for another puppy on the rescue websites. I am always reminded of how His timing is perfect & His plan is always a good plan!

Walking with God has been an amazing journey. He is always working on something new in us. I already know the next thing He is going to work on in me is my addiction to food. Food is a tough one, because we need food to live & it does not hurt anyone else if we are overeating & not taking care of ourselves physically. It is socially acceptable & so many things revolve around eating and the temptation is always there to make bad choices! I am currently on blood pressure medicine, heart disease & diabetes both run in my family. As I get older, I know that I may have health issues that occur because of my family history & my unhealthy eating & lifestyle. I know that God wants us to take care of our "temples" so that we can be in good health to carry out His plan for our lives. So, I am currently in the process of surrendering this area of my life to Him. I know that "with God.... all things are possible" & that through the power of His Word & with the help of the Holy Spirit that God will help me overcome this addiction & my bad eating habits.

I have also learned through CR how important it is for us to share our testimonies with others of what God has done in our lives. I do share how God has transformed my life with people I meet or when I reconnect with my past clients that I have not seen in years & I share it at The HUB each month, but I have not taken the time to write out my whole testimony out so I can share it @ CR Meetings. I have wanted to do it for years, because I know it's an important part of our journey's in Celebrate Recovery, but I kept putting it off. (Procrastination is one of my character defects) So I had mentioned to my sister a while ago that I really wanted to take the time to write my testimony out so I could share it on my 10-year sobriety anniversary May of 2021 at CR, but I kept putting it off & didn't start writing it.... until I received an email from Pete asking me if I would be interested in giving him a written copy of my testimony that he could put in a book that he is writing. He said that I could use my CR testimony if I had it written out. I knew when I got his email that this was GOD letting me know that I needed to stop procrastinating & start writing it, so I did. It took me longer than I thought it would, but it is finally finished!!

I wake up every day, thankful that God opened my eyes to the effects that alcohol had on my life. I had no idea how different life could be when we are truly living in a relationship with Him. "For the Kingdom of God is not a matter of eating & drinking, but of righteousness, peace and joy in the Holy Spirit." (Romans 14:17) I pray every day & ask God to help me to be more aware of His presence. I don't want to miss any of the ways that He interacts with me throughout the day whether it be through His beautiful creation or speaking to me through His Word or through one of His children. I pray & ask Him to use me to speak to others. If someone comes to mind and I believe it is God nudging me to reach out to them & check in with them or encourage them in some way. I also heard it said before that our life may be the only Bible that someone reads. I want others that do not know Jesus to come to know Him & to know the love that He has for them. And as Paul states in 2Cornithians 5:17 "We are Christ's ambassadors (that is His official representatives on earth) God is using us to speak to you: we beg you, as though Christ himself were here pleading with you, receive the love he offers you-be reconciled to God."

I will close with Romans 12:9-18 where Paul is giving us guidelines on how to live as Christians in this fallen world and to live out our faith every day.

"Be sincere in your love for others. Hate everything that is evil and hold tight to everything that is good. Be devoted to one another in brotherly love. Honor one another above yourselves. Share with God's people who are in need. Practice hospitality.

Bless those who persecute you, bless and do not curse. Rejoice with those who rejoice and mourn with those who mourn. Live in harmony with one another. Do not be conceited. Do not repay evil for evil. Be careful to do what is right in the eyes of everybody. If it is possible, as far as it depends on it, live at peace with everyone."

CHAPTER EIGHT

Steve Galegor, Jr

I have known of Steve and his ministry for many years. It has been in the past 10 years or so we have connected at various functions sponsored by the Fellowship of Grace Brethren Churches, now Charis Fellowship. I first knew of his father when he was serving in New Mexico years ago with Native Americans.

"Thus, if anyone is in the Messiah, there is a new creation! Old things have gone, and look—everything has become new!

It all comes from God. He reconciled us to himself through the Messiah, and he gave us the ministry of reconciliation. This is how it came about: God was reconciling the world to himself in the Messiah, not counting their transgressions against them, and entrusting us with the message of reconciliation. So we are ambassadors, speaking on behalf of the Messiah, as though God were making his appeal through us. We implore people on the Messiah's behalf to be reconciled to God." (The Kingdom NT)

- 2 Corinthians 5:17-20

Being an ambassador and representing 'another' as a reality and experience was made pretty clear to me as a kid growing up in a family that followed Christ. I knew early on that my parents, Steve and Chris, had come to know Jesus as a young married couple, and their love for Him and desire to follow and serve set an agenda for who we were as a family and for my identity and purpose even as a young child. It was who we were and what we did with our lives. Like most kids growing up in that situation, I assumed this was the norm for most families, though perhaps in slightly different ways.

The church family and the relationships that we had there as a family were the primary people I got to know and relate to outside of my own immediate and extended family. These were the people we spent free time with if we could and that seemed to be often what we did after meeting with the church on Sundays at lunch or in the evenings. Life was tied to this community in personal ways, but sort of the norm of things, and nothing really personal for me in terms of my knowing and following Christ.

It was through the church families that the Lord got my attention at an early age. While I was very young, and don't clearly remember the sequence of events, I do remember the sadness and grief when a toddler in the church, a little girl about my sister's age passed away in her sleep from 'crib death' (SIDS). I remember the pain and the grief going on around me and realized that this new experience could indeed become reality in our own household. That was made even more clear when some of the little girl's Christmas gifts appeared under the tree that year but now for my own sister.

I just remember being struck by the brutal reality and pain of death, loss and separation. I was inwardly despondent and terribly frightened by the prospect of being torn away from my own family, particularly my parents, by sudden tragedy. This, coupled with the first funeral I remember for my maternal great grandmother who I had seen alive but now was faced with the choice as a little boy to see her lying in a casket along with the family, or to remain with my cousins at the house while the adults remembered her. I chose the latter and didn't regret it, but the sharp emotions of the situation remained. As parents are keen to do, my father saw this and came alongside my bed one night asking what was wrong and what was going on inside. I shared my awful fear of separation from them, and he shared the hope was not final because of Jesus and His death in my place. It brought healing and peace immediately, and I remember speaking to God in a conscious and personal way that night beside my bed gazing at the stars in the vastness of space outside my windows. I began to know the king I would come to follow more and more and represent with life for and to others.

Middle school and high school years meant lots of moves while dad was making the courageous and hard moves to obey the Lord with his life in preparation for ministry. Church life and family remained central and vital, as that was where the supportive and encouraging instruction and relationships were connected to the same Lord and savior I had come to know as a small child. Those friends were closer than most I had at school or in the neighborhood because of our common faith. There was a special bond there and kind and committed adults constantly challenging me to live what I believed, no matter what the cost. Those years at Pleasant View Community Church and then Winona Lake Grace Brethren Church were absolutely foundational. Being baptized by Charles Ashman along with family to the many friends, quiz teams, shared sports events and honest challenges in youth group motivated me to live authentically for Jesus wherever and whenever. Men like Dan Michaels, Ed Lewis and Dave Bogue left a lasting impression on the opportunity to and the joy of representing Jesus and His family, my church family, well before the watching world.

The Lord used believers at school to challenge me as well to be an example to my peers for the Lord. Here was my field in which to live a distinctive kind of life, but not in a weird way rather an attractive one. There were always the pressures of the peer group, but knowing the family I came from, the church family I represented and the Jesus my friends needed the joy of knowing was always before me. I was not perfect, but I was called to be an ambassador in a world that was getting bigger as the years went on. At that age I knew that would be what I was to do no matter where I ended up and whatever I did with the life ahead, and it was important to do anything and everything with my best effort, as if I were doing it for Jesus. I really believed I was.

College at Ball State University made the world even bigger and now with a lot more choices and freedom to observe the options that lay before me. I had chosen a career path via the college of architecture there and was confident this was where the Lord would have me as his ambassador going forward. I had a long interest and desire to build things, much in the likeness of my maternal grandfather and through the shaping of a few teachers and a mentor in Ralph Hall who worked in the office a few doors down from my fathers at what was then 'Home Missions' for the Fellowship of Grace Brethren Churches. I found a group of Christ-oriented friends in the first days of school and maintained those connections throughout my five years of degree work there. One unassuming young lady, who was often on the other side of the group, found herself eating breakfast with me one morning in the winter of 1987 when all the others had scurried off to class. That led to a first date just before Valentine's Day and engagement and marriage three years later when Melanie finished her degree with one more left for me in my five-year degree.

Melanie and I had talked long into many nights about what I believed and the life orientation toward Christ I had followed to date, and her family was faithfully involved in a local church in their hometown of Crawfordsville in west central Indiana. During those years, my own parents made the huge step of faith to leave the stability of the home and life we had built in Northern Indiana to move to New Mexico to join the Grace Brethren work with Native American brethren. The world got bigger again as my wife and I spent time out there and met people and experienced a world very different from the one we had grown up in. That world was new, strange, but left the impression that there was more to representing Christ in familiar places but could and should be done in strange places as well. Spending our first months in marriage in Santa Fe stretched us, but it was for a short three-month time, caused us to seek the encouragement of a church family, and in a way, preparing us for something we would not come to understand for a number of years yet.

Our last year at Ball State was one of forging married life together, thinking ahead and preparing for next steps, wherever that would be. I knew and wanted it to be out West somewhere, as I had carried a dream in my heart since being a kid of living in the mountains out West, particularly Colorado. My wife agreed to this, our first adventure together for the long haul and her first time far from the home she grew up in and the family that was so dear to her and was becoming increasingly dear to me as well as my 'second family'. We settled in Fort Collins, Colorado, about as idyllic a place as I could imagine, with a job with a uniquely positioned, internationally recognized landscape architecture and planning firm. We were starting simple, but in a place that we began to love, and soon, people would be added to that fondness in our church home at Faith Church. As God often does, we encountered those in his family of our peer group who would warmly welcome us and immediately draw us into a community of young marrieds like ourselves who were starting off in life and career together, wanting to do that in a way that served Jesus as best we could.

We enjoyed this new world of ours in Colorado and took it all in as best we could at the time in the midst of the challenge of making ends meet, as all do in the early years of marriage. The church moved quickly to the center of our lives and relationships, and it was on one Sunday night as we were going about our usual routine that a student ministries leader, originally from Colorado's Western slope, who was working in Eastern Europe had just returned from participating with one of the first groups of foreigners and Americans who had been allowed into formerly Communist Albania. That was December of 1991, and the country had just had its first elections in March of that same year. Don Mansfield challenged the church to send a team of ten from our church to work alongside student groups that would be blitzing the country with the gospel, particularly in tandem with English speaking students from the university there who were turning to the Lord and acting as interpreters for others coming with the message of Jesus. Thousands were showing up to see the Jesus film where only hundreds could fit. Conversations with people on the street led quickly to inquiries about getting a Bible in the Albanian language. I was intrigued, captivated and caught by the uniqueness of it all, but it also awakened a memory that laid dormant for a while, and I shared it with my wife when we stopped to buy milk on the way home that night and told her that for some reason, I needed to go and be on that team.

"You're crazy", she replied, "we just got here, no one even knows who we are, but go ahead and try." Why the strong urge at that point? I spent many an evening watching the sun go down over the corn and bean fields to the West wanting to follow it and see what was still being illuminated by it 'out there' somewhere. I had devoured the monthly subscription we had to National Geographic that came to our home as a kid growing up in Northern Indiana, the yearly Christmas gift from our grandparents who themselves had gone to some interesting parts of the world. In October of 1980, when I was in sixth grade, the first and only mention I had ever seen about a place called Albania was featured in a short article laced with photos about this tiny nation in Southeast Europe. 'Albania Alone Against the World' was the headline. I still have the magazine. Indeed, it had been, given what I had just heard from the gentleman speaking and raising the need that night. Guests were now welcome, and, seemingly, those with the news of the world's Creator known as Jesus, in this, the world's only officially atheist nation since 1967.

I had worked with and been a part of student ministry during our years at Ball State, so I was already familiar with the message and methods we would be using. That was likely one of the reasons I was asked as a very young man to go with the team of ten in the summer of 1992 for three weeks of 'beach evangelism'. The world was about to get a lot bigger and more interesting as an ambassador of king Jesus. This first time outside my own country was not to be forgotten in almost every way. The poverty and brokenness were staggering and unimaginable for me. The warmth and nature of the people stood in stark contrast to the brutal remnants of the communist world they had been forced to build. Their curiosity about things I lived for in Christ was more than refreshing and invigorating, it awakened a hope I had for them that had never been so badly wanted or needed in my home country. Who were these people and what had happened here? To my surprise there they were in Paul's letter to the Romans in chapter 15. Illyricum – the Latin word for the land of the hard to subjugate 'free people'. I had to actually go there to learn about what had been in my own Bible all along. And God was now changing the history of the ancestors of those who had gotten the news about Jesus from Paul himself.

I returned home excited, dazed, and sick all at the same time. Because the one flight a week that was to take us home decided not to show up, I was now going to miss being the best man at my college roommate's wedding in Pennsylvania. I had not been able to keep food down for several days and had dropped about 20 pounds or so. Despite all that, I regretted nothing but knew something big was going on in a place that few people had ever heard of or been to. And I was a little proud of that perhaps in my growing interest in missions back at the church in

Colorado. I was going to go back and do this and that and...God decided to have me lose my job to an economic downturn but opened a door with the same firm in the San Francisco office. California, here we come!

The bay area was another new adventure, and hard to understand how we two young kids from Indiana made our way through that move. We had each other, but my wife was now a long way from family, and I was a long way from where I thought and felt life should be going. Next step? Find a church, and that's what we did in those first days living in Walnut Creek. Like we had at Faith in Ft. Collins, we connected with the young marrieds groups and had a huge number of friends within weeks. "How was that possible?" my coworkers in the city would ask over breaks when I told them I had helped paint the house of one of these new friends over the weekend past. We discovered very quickly that one couple of the group also lived in our little apartment complex on the other side of the pool and that relieved us, being that we were likely one of the few native-born families living in the sea of cultures there. We settled in and began to think about starting a family; it seemed like the time.

Albania had become a good memory in the rear-view mirror of life at that point until a visiting interim pastor from Scotland spoke at a Saturday morning men's breakfast about this tiny little country, he and no one he knew really knew about. I recognized faces in the photos. I calmly and gratefully went up to him afterward and thanked him for sharing, as I had seen and experienced the same kinds of things in my time there. He looked at me intently and declared something like, "that's great because I sense that you will be going back there." That would be nice, I thought, but not really in the cards. However, I kept it in my mind as we prepared to join my parents for a camping trip around Durango, Colorado in just a short time. We decided to make a trip up to Fort Collins as well; we were in the state anyway and enjoyed the drive through the heart of the Rockies. We met with church friends and I stopped by my old office to say hello. I saw the principal partner who took me aside into his office and asked quickly if I would consider a move back, with twice the salary and moving expenses taken care of. You can guess what our response was on the spot.

Back in Colorado we settled in again and waited for the birth of Jonah that coming Fall. We went right back into the previous church family and found our place among the same friends who were now having kids of their own. A second team had just returned from Albania, and a new pastor there, Don McReavy, was developing a strategy and plans for training in the church that promised to be a help to the fledging churches and believers in Albania too. The church was connecting with Albanian immigrant believers, some we had known back in 1992. All great to be part of and to observe, but I had lost the fervor I had had before from the first trip, though blessed to see the church continuing. In that capacity, I was invited to become part of a serious and significant leadership and theological training that was taking root in the church. My world, life and ministry were about to become God-sized, and the true nature of being an ambassador of King Jesus would emerge for us.

The studies seemed strange and complicated with no easy or obvious answers. We were studying the book of Acts and then Paul's letter and then 'sound teaching', but it wasn't a mastering of information but deep thinking, and outside the box at that. Lots of reading and writing was enabled and encouraged by the whole group who were doing this voluntarily at 5:30 in the morning every Thursday before work. I liked to learn, had always appreciated theology and study from dad's seminary days and the numerous profs of his who populated the churches I grew up in. But something was different here, and I couldn't put my finger on it. Through persistence and struggle, the light came on and got brighter – to be a Christian was not a personal, pious experience with Jesus as my guru alongside others. This was the 'center' of Christ's plan for all nations and times. This was what I had been saved into and what Jesus meant in the Great Commission. Not merely go and share the good news with everybody but go and make disciples in and through these pockets of new humanity to the ends of the earth. That is what the Apostles had done and Paul in particular. His letters weren't written *to me*, but they were *for me* and us today, not so that I could be an exceptionally spiritual person, but were tools to found, shape and sustain those churches, and that was the real story and purpose that framed in my identity and life purpose. I had seen and experienced this in countless ways in my life to date through the church, and now I clearly knew why and had a vague notion at that point as to what to do about it.

Our oldest, Jonah, was born that fall, and I was already in a state of tension with the things I had been learning and become convinced of well into the next year of 1994. By the end of that year, my wife, Melanie, had caught it by the osmosis of discussion and thinking out loud together so much so that, when the church leadership approached us about a defined time of service toward church planting in Albania, it didn't seem terribly implausible. Hard and uncertain? Yes, but we could get our hearts and minds around it, and it made sense with the tension I felt and the things I had learned, was still learning and deeply committed to continue learning no matter what lay ahead in life. With that and a strategy set by and committed to fully by the church leaders, we were sent to Albania in the fall of 1995 along with a dear colleague, Aida Raider, who had herself committed to a 'second career' mission at this time when she should be retiring and enjoying family.

It would take a whole other volume and work to give full detail to those five years in Albania from 1995 to 2000. By God's grace, I will do that someday, if only to leave behind a record of all that happened and what we stored up in our hearts and minds to our children and grandchildren. Our second, Emma, was born during a furlough back in Colorado and then grew to a toddler in the years remaining in Albania. Needless to say, the idea of being 'ambassadors' for King Jesus was now in the fullest mode we had ever imagined. We were to help establish embassies here in the 'Paris of the Balkans,' the city of Kortcha, where we now found ourselves with a multinational team of missionaries, all working with the same church movement, growing up around one of the only lights for the gospel that existed prior to the darkness of the years of atheist Communism. What a hard and challenging time that was to work alongside those dear people. The Albania of those days hardly exists anymore with all the change that has happened. It lives fondly with us and became the foundation for our next assignment as ambassadors of the new creation Jesus had inaugurated. We also now knew and learned from many fellow ambassadors of Albanian origin whose new devotion to the true Lord of the world inspired and motivated us to be His representatives among their countrymen in a place where they could not easily go, but we could, the great cities of the Northeastern United States that were collecting new immigrants from Albania by the droves and no specific witness existing among them.

Through the church once again as his central focus, God had made the connection with our sending church in Colorado and a large church in the city of New York, who was wrestling through the same courses I had done and which had radically reshaped my understanding of mission, the church, leadership development, discipleship, relief and development, etc. Over barbeque lunch in Ames, Iowa, in the spring conference of the BILD International Network, a casual conversation of what was 'going on' in Colorado and New York City led to an email that showed up in my inbox in Albania and an airplane ticket for the end of May to go visit New York City and see if an ambassador was needed there for one of the most populous concentrations of Albanians outside their homeland. Here we knew the language and culture of these unique people and perhaps there was an opportunity to extend the work there. Indeed, there was, and just as the early ambassadors, like Paul and his team, often got reassigned to new needs, so we set out with two little kids to go to the place considered the center of the world, where literally all the world's ambassadors gather to deal with the affairs of the nations. The world was going to get bigger again, but what to do and how to do the affairs of the King was getting clearer and coming more sharply into focus.

Once again, a church home was waiting for us with open arms, and under the direction of Dan Mercaldo we were greeted and welcomed to be part of the ministry team at Gateway Cathedral and to begin developing the plans and vision for representing Jesus and multiplying His family among the Albanians of Staten Island. It was wonderful to have that place and to receive the love and care we needed after five very tough years in a unique cross-cultural setting. However, we were still in one, but with many advantages both from studies and experience, and also through a web of relationships and contacts we couldn't have put together on our own. God had been doing things up to that point and there was a wide-open field before us unlike anything we had experienced to that point. Like the Albanians themselves, we were new immigrants to this place, a city which is also a like a country in and of itself, that happens to be attached to the North American continent. With the events of 9-11 the year after we moved there, we also came to understand how cities like it become places with the best of humanity and the worst of humanity all in one place. It too was a place in our homeland to learn to be ambassadors among the nations that are gathered there. There was always a sense of that, and you never left it. In one moment, you were speaking Albanian and living in that world, the next you were buying milk from the Indian owned grocery down the block.

We made our presence and intentions known through the service of helping Albanians grasp and become comfortable with the English language and the ways of our own country. Albanians had done the same for us during our five years there and it was all about the goal of developing a network of 'families of families; wherever we could, and God would lead. Our last child, Caleb, was born during our time in the city and really added to our family in a way that we never thought – we were now 'outnumbered' as parents but in a wonderful way for the dynamic of our family. With the help of others who caught the idea of 'ambassadorship,' the Brooklyn Albanian church family began in the home of a new believer who approached me after an event and asked that because he had heard I started churches would I come and start one in his home. We used our own home to begin to bring the church more central to our own life and family with a mix of American and Albanian family who remain active with us to this day. Circumstance shifted our base from Staten Island to Northern New Jersey in 2004, all rooted in the centrality of Christ's plan for the church and the church family at Grace Church in Clifton, where we found a new home and base to also assist a work among the many Albanians in North New Jersey that had been started by a colleague in 2002. That precipitated our move to New Jersey in 2008 that has been home to us ever since and provided the stability and strength of an entire church who has seriously bound themselves to our stewardship and realized new opportunities that we have stepped into together as Christ's emissary for reconciling us to one another and the world to Him, right in our neighborhood where 84 languages can be identified in the local high school.

It became clear to me in the move from Albania to home that Paul and others on his team like him were the prototypical ambassadors he speaks of in 2 Corinthians 5. An ambassador who is competent and trusted takes on a wider sphere of ministry that can only be created within a larger 'grand strategy' and the maturity that time and experience alone can create. This compelled me to define and give shape to ongoing work among Albanians, not in a single locale but in the wider Diaspora and especially among Albanian and ex-pat colleagues still leading and developing churches back in Albania and Albanian-speaking Kosova that we had gotten to know well through refugees that stayed in our home in the spring of 1999. It seemed the time to begin to forge and develop a network of leaders and churches coming together around what Roland Allen once referred to as 'the Way of Christ and His Apostles'. This was shorthand for the inner logic of the New Testament, not as a series of books or theology manuals, but windows into the story of Jesus and the kingdom He inaugurated now in full view through a network of spontaneously expanding local churches in the ancient Mediterranean world. With this plan as a prototype, we could not only strengthen our own work, but band together in substantive ways to get the gospel to Albanians as far away as Melbourne, Australia to points in between, being the 'global tribe' that they are due to technology today and ease of travel. They are more connected today than the brothers of yesteryear living on two sides of the same mountain with an international border running between them. What a unique time in which to learn and work together to be ambassadors.

Melanie and I remain in New Jersey these days, though the kids are grown and moving on to other places. Jesus' plan and grand strategy through the church remains the same and has taken me to France, Holland, Ukraine, Greece and numerous other places. As I look back, indeed all things have become new, and they continue to be renewed by God's grace in the lives of individual people and the opportunities presented. I sat for coffee in Manhattan yesterday with a believer from Kosova who is new to the country, knows many of the people that I also know back home, and is set on seeing his young family settled into a church, something which he misses so badly as a believer. Perhaps we will see a new work in his home in the Bronx among 40,000 Albanians there? Maybe. In the end, I look back at the words of Paul the model ambassador who said that "It all comes from God. He reconciled us to himself through the Messiah, and he gave us the ministry of reconciliation." What lies ahead for us, in looking back over our lives as I have, truly convinced me that what lies ahead will be much, much more of the same in new and fresh ways.

Steve Galegor, Jr.
April 14, 2021 – Clifton, New Jersey

CHAPTER NINE

Shannon Horst

I just recently met Shannon for the first time earlier this year, in 2021. He was referred to me by a mutual friend to discuss faith-based recovery. I was impressed by the transparency and willingness to "bare-all" during our first meeting. Not only was he incredibly open but I sensed a sincere desire to pull anything from our time that might help him overcome his sense of failure. He is a humble man who encouraged me by his desire to not give up, continue fighting regardless of his past failures. I believe he has a story to tell you may find encouraging.

No one ever wakes up one day and decides to self-destruct. Instead, the road to self-destruction is paved with small compromises, patterns of behavior fueled by wrong belief, and unfortunate choices. I've seen this to be the case in my own life.

In 2012, I was called to serve as the pastor of a small church in Ohio. It seemed as if all my preparation had finally paid off. I remember when I walked into my study for the first time, thinking that I had made it. My dream of leading a congregation had become a reality. So, with great ambition and naivety, I set out to "change the world". Some wonderful things happened over the years I served that congregation. At the same time however, there were gut-wrenching disappointments and heartaches. Things that Bible College never could have prepared me for. I always had great respect for the Word of God, and I was in it every day. As time passed, I began to sacrifice my personal devotion time for sermon preparation. Both aspects of study are very important, however trying to feed others without first feeding yourself is spiritually draining. It is strange but I began to look at Scripture as something that was meant for others, and I ignored my own need for it. It was not long before I found my desire to please the people of the church taking center stage in my mind. And with every set back that occurred I felt like more and more like a failure. I always wanted to please people and to seek their approval. I've struggled with that for as long as I can remember, and it seemed as if my position in the church only served to fuel that terrible desire. Negative "self-talk" became a regular aspect of my internal dialogue. I've often said that, if Satan whispered in my ear with a demonic voice, I would know that is was not to be trusted. However, he whispered using my voice, a voice I did trust. My internal dialing coupled with the growing difficulty of leading a church through some significant change made it all but impossible to sleep. I would lay in bed for hours replaying every failure, every missed opportunity, and every conversation. I had to find a way to cope, and quiet the internal voice of condemnation that I was fighting against. Instead of pursuing healthy methods, I began to drink. Just in the evenings, I told myself that it was only to take the edge off so that I could sleep. It was one of those small compromises in life that serve to take you off track. Trying to gain affirmation from man, was destroying me. As the stress increased, so did the negative self-talk. As the negative self-talk increased, so did my drinking to cope with it all. After four years of ministry the strain became too much, and I resigned. The resignation, however, did very little to quell the feelings of worthlessness. I felt defeated and lonely. Shame crept in. All I could think about is how I squandered such a remarkable opportunity that The Lord gave me. I remember very vividly, being terrified to call my father and tell him that I had failed. I disappointed so many already, I really did not want to add him to the list. But of course, after we spoke, he showed me nothing but love and support.

The month after I resigned from the church, I was alarmed to find a lump on the right side of my neck. The following month I was told it was cancer, nothing prepares you for that news. After what felt like a defeat at the hands of Satan in my ministry, I was faced with disease. I was scared, and in crept the familiar face of depression. It felt as if my world was falling apart. First my career ended, and then it appeared that my life was soon to follow.

What followed was several surgeries, months of treatment and a pervasive sense of shame and guilt. I felt alone and confused. I knew the "right" things to say, I knew how I would respond to a church member in my situation. But it all seemed so trite. I continued to self-medicate with alcohol and pain medication as a way of escape. I could not stop the physical or mental pain any other way, so I masked them. An acquaintance of mine came to visit me because he saw my battle with cancer on social media. He warned me of the dangers of opioid addiction, and he offered an alternative. He had somehow obtained medical marijuana and presented it as a safe option. It made sense to me, and my friend agreed to get me a regular supply. After all, who would want to be addicted to opioids. However, in the weeks and months that followed, not only did I self-medicate with alcohol and pills I added marijuana to the equation. I began to withdraw from my family even more. Most nights I was in bed by seven, barely coherent because of the mix of drugs in my system. I did anything I could to hide from social situations. This went on for nearly two years. Finally, one day my wife had had enough. She put her foot down and demanded that I get help.

September 11, 2018 with the help of some concerned friends, I checked into the Bethesda Men's Shelter in Harrisburg. The mission is a homeless shelter that happens to have a drug and alcohol rehab program as well. Overcome with shame and guilt I climbed the stairs to my humiliation. I could not help but think about how far I fell. It was not that long ago that I was looked to for spiritual counsel and yet there I was. I had one change of clothes, going through the intake process, and waiting to move into my new home in a shelter. The first few days were spent in self-loathing, 'how could this have happened?'. Again, I felt alone, abandoned in a strange place surrounded by the homeless. I was out of my element to say the least.

As I began to acclimate myself to the schedule, I began to see hope. Through Bible study, prayer and counseling I began to understand the root of my addiction. I saw that I had built up idols, seeking man's approval rather than God's. This idolatry set me up for failure every time. I remember my counselor's words well and they still sting, "Shannon" he said, "you're not an alcoholic, you're an idolater". Addiction was just a symptom of a far deeper problem. Confessing my idolatry was freeing. The shelter that once felt like a prison, was beginning to feel like a hospital. It became a place of healing. I formed deep friendships with some of the men there, relationships that I would have never otherwise had. I remember years ago, praying that the Lord would open my eyes to the hurting. I prayed that the Lord would give me opportunities to reach the "least of these". Years later, I found myself literally among them. The catch though, was *I was one of them*. I was not a "white knight" riding in to save them, I was broken and hurting just like them. My time at Bethesda was invaluable, and I count it as one of the most valuable experiences I have ever had. I saw the Gospel not only as something to be proclaimed to others, but as a soothing balm for my own soul. My counselor once said that I was good at reading Scripture, but he followed with "you're not very good at allowing Scripture to read you". It is a subtle difference, but his words impacted me deeply. During my time in the mission, I began reading the Word differently. Reading the Word prayerfully. Pleading with the Lord to allow His Word to penetrate my own heart first, before trying to disperse it to others.

When I returned home, I found it to be a completely different place than the one I left. My behavior of the previous years had damaged my marriage and drove a wedge between me and my two oldest children. Yes, there is healing from addiction, but there will always be consequences. It was not long before I was asked to leave the house for good. So, I found myself homeless once again. I lived in my pickup for a little over two weeks, then my parents took me in for a time until I found the apartment that I live in now. I have been completely sober since September 11, 2018 and with the Lord's help I will stay that way. I have begun discovering different coping mechanisms to remain in recovery. As strange as it seems, the most effective way I've found is: vulnerability. So much of my life in ministry was spent hiding my emotions, telling people I was "fine" when

I was far from it. Certainly, there is a balance to this, but I have been intentional about sharing my weaknesses with others. I have a new appreciation for what Paul wrote, "But he said to me, "My grace is sufficient for you, for my power is made perfect in weakness." Therefore, I will boast more gladly of my weaknesses, so that the power of Christ may rest upon me" (2 Corinthians 12:9). I once made my life about showing people how strong and capable, I was, it's no wonder that I could not sustain the illusion. Paul was most effective when he admitted his weaknesses and leaned into the strength of the Lord. When we humble ourselves enough to admit that only the Lord can sustain us we're given great freedom and power. In our brokenness, we are most effective. I have also come to understand that I cannot do this alone. So, I have surrounded myself with trusted friends who are invested in my life and in my sobriety. This seems to be a by-product of vulnerability. When I started opening to friends and family, I found that they naturally wanted to support me. It seems that it not only "takes a village to raise a child" but it takes a village to support an addict. And I will forever be grateful for my village.

Through it all I still feel compelled to preach the Gospel of Jesus Christ. I pray that one day He would see fit to place me in vocational ministry once again. Where once I saw shame and failure, now I see preparation through pain. The experiences that I have had and the pain that I have felt has uniquely qualified me to reach others who may be feeling as hopeless as I once did. When I came to the end of myself, broken, living in a homeless shelter I was comforted by the Lord. Now I see that those experiences and the comfort I found was given to me so that I might comfort others in the same way. The Apostle Paul spoke of this very thing in 2 Corinthians 1:3-4 (ESV), "Blessed be the

Acknowledgements

I want to take a minute to thank each person who authored their own chapter. It took over a year of reminders, nudging and lots of prayers to get it all together. I also want to thank my friend Raymond Marusi who has been a prayer and financial partner with this project. My wife Brenda for her patience enduring the times spent at my desk. Thankfully, we are on the same page about time spent serving God.

CPSIA information can be obtained
at www.ICGtesting.com
Printed in the USA
BVHW030337260821
614918BV00001B/53